"The holy grail of data is when you d
of your own organization. *Data Leverage* provides excellent, practical
guidance on how to dissect, understand, and implement your ideal data
partnership strategy."

—Sharon Rowlands
President, USA Today Network Marketing Solutions
and CEO, ReachLocal

"There can be no book more packed with practical, common sense
guidance than *Data Leverage*. It is a must-read at every level in
every industry."

—Bob Herrmann
President & CEO, Discovery Data

"Data is like electricity for businesses: essential to almost every aspect
of its operations, but deadly if mishandled. Although data partnerships
increase the potential reward, most companies are paralyzed by the
increased risk. In *Data Leverage*, the Ward brothers have created a
manual to help you understand the opportunity, navigate the minefield
of risks, and unlock the value of data partnerships."

—Dave Frankland
co-author of Marketing to the Entitled Consumer

"We have ways to qualify and employ key personnel. We have ways to
qualify and select physical assets. Yet we have lacked a practical process
for qualifying and capitalizing on data itself. This is where *Data Leverage*
comes in."

—Sean R. McMahon, PhD
Doherty Emerging Professor of Entrepreneurship, Elon University

DATA
LEVERAGE

Unlocking the surprising growth potential of data partnerships

Christian J. Ward & James J. Ward

WARD PLLC • MIAMI • 2019

Data Leverage
Unlocking the surprising growth potential of data partnerships

by Christian J. Ward & James J. Ward

Published by Ward PLLC
1101 Brickell Avenue
Miami, Florida 33131
(305) 302-6909

Distributed by SourceMedia
1 State Street Plaza 27th Floor
New York, New York 10004
www.sourcemedia.com

SourceMedia.

Copyright © 2019 Ward PLLC. All rights reserved.

ISBN: 978-1-7329917-0-5 trade paperback
978-1-7329917-1-2 electronic book
978-1-7329917-2-9 audiobook

LCCN: 2018914586

DataSmart and DataSmart Method are trademarks of Ward PLLC.

Other trademarks are the property of their respective owners.

Editing: Josh Bernoff

Copyediting: Linda Pruessen

Index: Josh Bernoff

Design and composition: www.dmargulis.com.

Cover design: Stephani Finks

First printing

MANUFACTURED IN THE UNITED STATES OF AMERICA

Contents

Foreword

I AM NOT A NUMBER, I am a free man!" So says the main character of the dystopian television series *The Prisoner*, an ex-spy played by Patrick McGoohan who is kidnapped and then trapped in a constantly surveilled community from which he can never escape. But he is wrong. He is a number. He is Number Six. And we never learn his name.

We are all numbers now. We are birthdays, credit scores, auto registrations, online purchase histories, bank records, Web searches, social media posts, and location histories. We are data. This data helps companies serve us. And, treated with appropriate care and in aggregate, the same data can enrich the companies that collect it. Data is the currency and competitive advantage that drives the future. But getting at that value is far from straightforward.

There is great potential here for every organization, as well as great risk. You cannot tap the value of this data without a guide. Furthermore, you must respect your obligations to the consumers from whom that data originates. You cannot treat them and their data as prisoners like Number Six.

Christian and Jay Ward have created the guide you need to safely, efficiently profit from data while respecting the rights of those the data describes. Their guide is based on vast experience. It is indispensable.

As an analyst and editor for over 20 years, I've seen technology trends come and go. I've watched companies embrace — and often screw up — their approach to ecommerce, to social media, to mobile technology, and to artificial intelligence. It's difficult to see the future clearly when you are barreling headlong into it. With this clouded vision, it's very easy to make mistakes in what appears to be uncharted and promising territory.

But this book is about far more than a technology trend — and will be relevant far longer. From the minute I encountered this text, I knew there was something special about it. The value of an organization's data is obvious and fundamental, a value that other technology trends only serve to enhance as they generate new forms of data. But unlocking that value? No one had ever before taken a broad and practical viewpoint on that topic.

This text comes from Christian and Jay's broad, deep experience with real companies. Where there is uncertainty, it provides reassurance. Where there is opportunity, it provides roadmaps. And where there is risk, it provides tools to protect yourself and your data subjects. With it, you can confidently and safely pursue the value of your data and negotiate on an even footing with partners much bigger, more experienced, and more savvy than yourself.

Data Leverage is a unique asset. Once you read what's here, you'll never see the world the same way again. More importantly, you'll be able to profit from it.

Now get to work.

Josh Bernoff
December 2018

DATA
LEVERAGE

Understanding Data Partnerships

TO PARAPHRASE JANE AUSTEN, it is a truth universally acknowledged that a company with valuable data must be looking for a data partnership.[1] Every business, regardless of size, generates and accumulates data in the course of its operations — data about customers, products, and competitors, and about the business itself. For many years, we treated this data as an economic byproduct of the main event of manufacturing, selling, or serving. But once automated processing of this data became widespread and cheap, businesses began to fully understand how information was a new form of currency. To profit from the enormous industry that data has become, companies must now apply leverage to maximize the value of that currency.

Data partnerships are now at the center of the most successful business strategies.

Data partnerships and the strategies that companies use to create and exploit them now determine which companies become successful. What do we mean by a data partnership?

A data partnership is the sharing of specific, identifiable data between two or more parties who mutually agree on a structure to leverage and protect the value of the data.

Facebook, Uber, Snapchat, Airbnb, Amazon, and thousands of other companies have leveraged data partnerships and data sharing agreements to create enormous value and opportunity.

---

1 Jane Austen, *Pride and Prejudice* (1813). You were supposed to read this in high school but probably didn't. It was good, in a *Downton Abbey* kind of way.

Conversely, many great companies have harmed their own reputations with failed data partnerships by failing to protect and to be transparent about how they use data. When a data partnership is not transparent about how the parties have agreed to treat the data, reputations are at risk. Why? Because the single most common reason for lawsuits about data breaches and enforcement actions by regulators is that a company wasn't straightforward about what it did with the data it had.[2]

Organizations don't naturally develop an overall approach or a cohesive strategy around data partnerships. For many, data assets are an afterthought to normal business operations. This inevitably leads to those assets being underutilized, or worse, trapped in a corporate structure that leaves little flexibility to leverage them. For this reason, each company needs to take a proactive approach to its data partnership strategy.

Why Do You Need a Data Partnership Strategy?

If you speak with executives at a multibillion-dollar industry leader and then speak with small-business owners, you'll notice some striking similarities. They all know that there is an opportunity for a more proactive data approach, but they are convinced that they aren't properly positioned to take advantage of it. This pattern of thinking is common: you'll see it not only in your own company but also in many of the businesses you deal with. Highly successful companies, even ones with global operations, are sometimes paralyzed by a lack of a data strategy from the top down.

It doesn't have to be this way. Amazon is one of the most famous turnarounds in this regard. By now, Amazon's transformation from mere online bookseller to the world's leading infrastructure-as-a-service company is well documented. Amazon's AWS cloud services platform has completely changed the way companies manage, share, and integrate data. Amazon consciously transformed itself from selling copies of books to

---

2   To the point that the Federal Trade Commission, which is the lead US governmental agency handling privacy issues, has a website literally entitled "Enforcing Privacy Promises" (see www.ftc.gov/news-events/media-resources /protecting-consumer-privacy/enforcing-privacy-promises).

hosting and powering the websites and platforms of Netflix, SAP, Adobe, Pinterest, and millions of other businesses.

Why and how did they do this? Jeff Bezos drove this transformation with a memo to all of the company's business division leaders around 2002. The memo is detailed and granular but boils down to the following highlights.[3]

- All teams will henceforth expose their data and functionality through service interfaces.
- Teams must communicate with each other through these interfaces.
- There will be no other form of interprocess communication allowed: no direct linking, no direct reads of another team's data store, no shared-memory model, no backdoors whatsoever. The only communication allowed is via service interface calls over the network.
- It doesn't matter what technology they use. HTTP, CORBA, Pub/Sub, custom protocols — doesn't matter. Bezos doesn't care.
- All service interfaces, without exception, must be designed from the ground up to be externalizable. That is to say, the team must plan and design to be able to expose the interface to developers in the outside world. No exceptions.
- Anyone who doesn't do this will be fired.

There is certainly a lot more that went into this strategy, and the effort to transform Amazon took years, but it was Bezos's vision to enable data to be internally and externally accessible that created one of the most flexible and successful data partnership platforms ever. More importantly, the second-to-last bullet above is what created the ability for data partnerships to drive the value of the business forward. By making all data services and datasets externally available, Bezos and Amazon were setting up their data strategy for the future, which is what all businesses should be doing.

Over the last two years, we've seen some form of the following paragraph on a presentation slide at almost every data-focused conference

---

3   Steve Yegge, a former Amazon engineer, provided this synopsis of the Bezos memo in a move that nearly got him fired by his other billionaire boss, Sergey Brin (Rip Empson, "How to Pitch Jeff Bezos [and Other 'Giant-Brained Aliens']," TechCruch, October 22, 2011, https://techcrunch.com/2011/10/22/how-to-pitch-jeff-bezos/).

attended. The quote has been stolen, and re-stolen, from a TechCrunch article by Tom Goodwin, in which he said:

> Uber, the world's largest taxi company, owns no vehicles. Facebook, the world's most popular media owner, creates no content. Alibaba, the most valuable retailer, has no inventory. And Airbnb, the world's largest accommodation provider, owns no real estate. Something interesting is happening.[4]

Each of those companies has created massive value by crafting data partnership approaches and then delivering a value greater than any one dataset could provide on its own. This is data innovation, combined with masterfully executed consumer marketing and user experience. Each one embraced the Amazon vision of open data structures, internally and externally, to power their go-to-market value proposition. In other words, when it comes to data partnerships, the whole is often greater than the sum of its parts.

Uber, for example, has taken a mashup of location data, points-of-interest data, GPS signals from cell phones running its app, driver app signals, weather, and traffic route information to build an incredibly disruptive service. Each one of those datasets existed before Uber, and many of them were available for free or at limited cost from one or more platforms. But it was Uber's ability to build meaningful partnerships to access the data it didn't have and then integrate it with internal data that figuratively and literally drove Uber's growth.

The same can be said for Amazon, Alibaba, Airbnb, and even more companies that don't begin with the letter *A*. Their approach to data isn't just a decision on which infrastructure to use or how to speed it up. Their approach is about accessing as much data as possible and using that access to create value. While your company may not be a global data powerhouse, remember, neither were any of these companies. However, at some point

---

4   Tom Goodwin, "The Battle Is for the Customer Interface," TechCrunch, March 3, 2015, https://techcrunch.com/2015/03/03/in-the-age-of -disintermediation-the-battle-is-all-for-the-customer-interface/.

in their existence, they made the decision to have a data partnership strategy, and so should you.

The DataSmart Method: Identify, Value, Structure, Protect

Thriving companies can, and must, identify their data assets. Put briefly, identification of data assets means understanding what information you have, and why it's useful. For some companies, this may be as simple as collecting customer lists, while for others it is a multifaceted inquiry into terabytes of data. But how companies identify data assets is a question of degree, and not activity. The task is often harder and more complex than you may expect, because your company may have preconceived notions about its data or may perpetuate fiefdoms that silo off data assets from each other. But with the right framework, you can simplify the process dramatically and bring some order to the chaos. This book is designed to help walk you through specific types of data assets and how to identify them. We will also present some exercises that should help uncover opportunities that aren't initially visible.

Once you have identified the company's data assets, you can begin the process of valuing them. Valuation is complex and subjective. You must properly tailor the process to whatever value criterion is ideal for your company. For example, many companies value their customer database above all else, even when someone could cheaply purchase almost every detail about a customer from a third-party vendor. What is the real value of data about your own customers? We'll describe that in some detail, because in many cases you can unlock the value not through the identification of a data asset, but by combining that dataset with additional, and often external, sources of information.

After a company has defined the data and put a preliminary value on it, it must create data partnership structures that will allow it to confidently utilize these assets in different strategies. Whether you are seeking to buy, sell, share, or resell data assets, you must consider some fundamental timing and legal approaches. The use or misuse of data often generates significant government, industry, regulatory, and even consumer perception risks; every company must understand each of these risks and how they affect partnerships. Equally important, the timing of when to utilize certain partnership structures is highly dependent on situational constraints, and so we will outline where and when to apply different tactics. The creation of partnerships is also the time for careful attention to details of contracts and other legal agreements regarding non-disclosure and confidentiality. It is crucial to get those agreements right from the outset, because there will not be time (or, often, money) to fix these problems later.

Once the data partnership is underway, the last step is to set up a reporting or feedback system to help protect not just the data assets but the value that access to those assets provides. Data is dangerously transferable, readily stolen or copied, and easily manipulated to disappear. We will talk about some of the more painful examples of this: not just external hackers attacking from the outside, but also the realization that a partnership you purposefully and excitedly signed somehow opened a backdoor for your data assets to walk out, never to be seen again. Focusing before and during a partnership negotiation on reporting requirements will help uncover these risks before they ever go into effect.

To recap, our approach is to identify your data assets, value them, structure the right data partnership strategy, and build a reporting framework to protect those assets. We will analyze this in two ways, integrating a business-savvy attention to maximizing value and a litigator's obsessive focus on protecting your business from legal liability.

We will help you answer questions like these:

- What data assets do you have?
- What is the value of data and having a strategy for partnership?
- How do you convey the value of your data?
- What do typical data partnerships have in common?
- What are the most common types of data partnerships?
- What are innovator partnerships?
- How do you identify mutually beneficial partnerships?
- What are reseller partnerships?
- What reporting and insights do I need in every data partnership?

As we analyze each of these questions and topics in depth, we will outline data partnership strategies and approaches to employ at different times in the life cycle of your business, depending on your objectives.

Two Perspectives on Data Partnerships

This book is designed to offer two perspectives, one from a data entrepreneur and the other from a data privacy litigator. We have found in our research that most discussions on data are either too dreamily opportunistic or too dreadfully restrictive. The reality lies somewhere between the perspective of the most starry-eyed entrepreneur and the most battle-hardened business litigator.

Christian Ward has had the unique experience of building data partnership strategies as an entrepreneur, an intrapreneur, an acquirer, a reseller, and, most importantly, as a participant in multiple industries. Working with some of the largest and most innovative companies in the world, he has crafted transformational data strategies that have positioned companies for success. Christian will share unique insights and pitfalls garnered from many different industries and situations.

As a litigator, James "Jay" Ward has a very different perspective. Jay has seen what happens when partnerships go awry and the consequences that come from a lack of planning. Every business relationship has its risks. But you can certainly mitigate the potential harm by thinking clearly about your goals, your assets, and your intended outcomes before signing an agreement with a data partner. Jay is an expert at crafting long-term data strategies that are more than simply finding this year's best partner. Jay focuses on understanding the value of, and the need to protect, the data you have, and the importance of complying with all of the privacy regulations that are so drastically changing the data landscape.

We have worked together closely, as, ideally, brothers should.

Throughout this book, we will highlight not only experiences across the topic of data partnerships, but also insights gained while working with some of the most respected data companies in the world. While every data partnership approach is unique, we'll share the most powerful commonalities, focusing on timing. Start-up, growth stage, and mature companies all have different needs based on the life cycle stage they are in, and their data strategies must track accordingly.

While the subject of data strategy often includes the topic of corporate data security, we won't be addressing technical security in detail, because there are already so many great books, classes, and articles on these subjects.

Lastly, it should probably go without saying, but this book isn't legal advice, and you need to consult with a lawyer before making any decisions that impact your legal rights. Instead, this book is a blueprint, a framework for how you should think about data partnerships and data strategy. Tailor your strategy to your own situation and retain appropriate legal representation.

What's in the Book

This book follows the DataSmart Method in both structure and content. In part I, we will walk through the data asset identification process. Part II focuses on both how to value your data assets and how to position them in a manner conducive to attracting strong partnerships. Part III will break down the most common structures of data partnerships and when to use each. And lastly, part IV will discuss how to protect your data assets through audits, reporting, and common legal frameworks.

Humility and Leadership Are Necessary to Succeed

There are two critical factors in any data partnership strategy: humility and leadership.

Many companies who don't think they have valuable data assets do, while those who overestimate their data assets don't. The problem is as much perception as it is attitude, and it will be a major determinant of your success. As a leader of your organization's data partnership approach, you should embrace a sense of humility that will open up creativity in your partnerships. Every different party you encounter who is interested in your data assets will value them from a unique perspective, one that will not perfectly align with your own. For this reason, learn to begin all of your dialogues in data partnership with an open mind that allows for creative ways to work with partners.

Remember, taking a humble attitude to a data partnership will help get things off on the right foot, but that doesn't mean you should be humble in the final contract and framework. Knowing your own data value, and the value of the other party's use of it, or vice versa, is much easier when your judgment is not clouded by a superior attitude.

The second critical factor of data partnership success is aligning leadership across your organization. Leadership at every level is required to make a data partnership strategy work. From the top down, every business unit must buy into the strategy and recognize its value and its risks. Without that alignment from leaders across the company, it is impossible to succeed; it is just too simple for even one person to sabotage the results. On countless occasions we have witnessed one leader seeking to wall off his or her portion of data, rather than opening it up to other opportunities, internal and external; this is enough to derail any strategy. Get leadership approval and alignment in terms as strong as possible (think of that Bezos memo) and we promise you will have what you need to succeed.

With that as a backdrop, let's begin with an understanding of what data is and the different viewpoints about its value and nature.

Part I: Identify

2

Data and People

WHAT IS DATA? Before we dive into data partnerships, structures, legal frameworks, and derivative use cases, we need a common definition of data and we must explore who owns it and who is responsible for it. You may think you know what data is, but before you plunge ahead, let's examine that understanding, why data merits protection, who regulates it, and what you can do to strike the appropriate balance between privacy and profitability.

We admit that we're nerds. That means our obsession with data, information, strategy, and law come together in a coherent bundle of geeky energy that we put to use for our clients. It also means we have a perspective on things that others typically do not share.

For example, we were recently discussing a document from CNIL, the French Data Protection Authority and remembered that, in French, the word *data* translates to *les données*, which is the plural of the word *donné*, which means "given." In fact, virtually every version of the word for data in European-based language revolves around that same concept: "this piece of information is what was given." The Latin *datum* means "having been given."

This is probably not how you think about data. For most of us, data just means information and, more specifically, electronically stored information. But all data is, in some sense, "given."

While not all data is about a person (weather data, for example, is not), the data that is most useful for partnerships typically will, in some way, relate back to a person. The weather data may help you predict purchasing habits for people, or the most efficient shipping method to reach an individual. So, while not all data is directly about individual persons, it is very common for all data to relate to, connect with, drive marketing to, or interact with an individual person.

Once you understand that all data is "given," it begs the question "who gave it?" In the midst of a data inventory or audit, it is very easy to think of the data as almost having created itself, or to see it as a dehumanized set of information that comes "from the internet." But that's not correct, of course. An individual person is the ultimate source of most of this information. Data itself, as mere information, has no rights, and our approach to the ethics of its use are going to depend substantially on the choices of the company processing it. But there are risks and benefits to dehumanizing, as opposed to humanizing, data.

The dehumanizing approach is the standard view in the United States. Data, unless otherwise required by law, is basically usable for any lawful purpose. You can't fabricate it and you can't lie about what you do with it, but as long as you got the data through legal means, it's yours to make use of. This structure has more or less facilitated the growth of Big Data, mass analytics, and algorithms so sophisticated they somehow know that you prefer Jimmy Cliff's version of "I Can See Clearly Now" to the more popular Johnny Nash rendition. Companies can dissect the data in the dehumanized approach in all its forms and endlessly repurpose it, creating new forms of value and new methods for reaching customers and growing business. The dehumanized approach is also a source of great stress for those same customers, and as a result, has caught the attention of regulators and politicians.

The humanized approach, by contrast, forces companies to recognize that a subject of data is a person with autonomy and rights. In Europe, data subjects have a fundamental right to their privacy, and that is why understanding the humanized approach to data is so essential. If you don't understand that the European General Data Protection Regulation (GDPR) is really about a completely different perspective on data, you're going to have a vastly more difficult time complying with it. For the European Union and for its Data Protection Authorities (DPAs), data is an extension of an individual, another aspect to their personhood. Yes, a person may have voluntarily given their data to a company to use, but that data will always belong to them because it is part of who they are.

Because this is the approach European regulators take, it is essential to understand the regulation; taking a "check the box" approach to the GDPR, or any other privacy regulation, isn't necessarily going to be enough. Think about what Věra Jourová, EU Commissioner for Justice, Consumers and Gender Equality, tweeted on April 9, 2018, about Facebook after the Cambridge Analytica scandal broke: "We will observe with great interest how the letter — and the spirit — of the law are applied." An American observer could be forgiven for saying, "Wait, what?" Complying with the letter of the law is one thing, but what's the spirit of the GDPR? Well, now you have your answer: the humanized approach.

With that in mind, you can see opportunities for US companies, and not just risk. It's clear that simply following pre-GDPR methods and practices will no longer suffice, and that we need to change our minds and change our approach to how we handle data. If nothing else, the torrent of data breach announcements each week should prove that. But you also can't try to run a business as if you were a regulator, because regulators aren't interested in profit.

There is a third way, a balance between the value of data and the rights of the data subject, which is a delicate balancing act. It requires an ongoing focus on how your business gathers and uses data, and how it interacts with the people who provide it. Your company's third way will never match anyone else's, because just as each datum is totally unique and data is universal, each business is trying to achieve success in its own way.

Aligning to New Data Opportunities

To dive in a little deeper to these differing perspectives on data, let's examine some unique and evolving datasets and review how they are gathered and utilized. We will then frame each one from both a humanized and dehumanized perspective to show that sometimes, even with the exact same dataset, the lens we use to view it can change the way we interpret the value and risk of the data.

Weather Data Partnerships

Weather has an unlimited number of possible interactions with businesses; we use weather data often in brainstorming sessions with clients. The weather may determine when to buy products, when to market them, when to put items on sale, when to raise prices (surge pricing for ride-hailing platforms leverage the weather, for example), even when to close business for the day. Accessing weather data as part of your data partnership strategy is a great way to open up your business to new concepts quickly.

For example, one national home improvement chain shifts their marketing spending based on the last five days of rainfall data plus the forecast for next five days of rainfall. To be clear, this is a humanized viewpoint in which a change in the weather affects the retailer's overall marketing approach at a zip code level of detail, not at the individual user level. In other words, by abstracting the weather data across a geographic region, the company wasn't targeting individual users. Instead, they leveraged a data partnership with a major weather data company to elevate marketing for products that address flooding, roof problems, drywall fixes, buckets, and tarps. This weather data partnership strategy led to substantial revenue increases.

On the other hand, weather apps have long tracked not only the weather but also the location of individuals utilizing their application on their phone. By default, most weather apps have "location services" turned on. In 2017, an investigative report uncovered that AccuWeather's app was tracking users even if the user had turned off "location services" in the application.[5] This enabled the app to track very specific data, and ultimately target individuals based upon their location. This approach to using weather data was a dehumanized approach, where the location of the subject and the weather affecting that subject was viewed as independent of the data subject's right to privacy.

---

5   Angela Fritz, "A Security Researcher Discovered AccuWeather App Tracked, Shared Your Location — Even If You 'Opt Out,'" *Washington Post*, August 27, 2017, https://www.washingtonpost.com/news/capital-weather-gang /wp/2017/08/23/security-researcher-discovered-accuweather-app-tracks-and -shares-your-location-even-if-you-opt-out/.

Marketing Lists and Append Partnerships

There are countless data companies such as Acxiom, Infogroup, Neustar, Dun & Bradstreet (D&B), Pitney Bowes,[6] and others that build partnerships around consumer data. They aggregate raw information like new home purchases with thousands of "propensity" models that let you buy leads and lists of prospective customers that fit into the "likes golf" or "active lifestyle" category. While it is common practice to buy this type of data or to pay to append it to your own customer list from your customer relationship management (CRM) system, data partnerships with these same firms are also available. Many of these same companies, through their aggregation agreements, will be open to you sharing some of your data with them to improve the quality of their content or to expand their breadth and depth with new data points.

There are real advantages here, although legally, you must have the rights to the data you are sharing in this type of relationship. Many businesses are starving for data sources that can improve their data quality or add some level of new unique qualifier, and they may agree to share data with you in a barter-style framework. We'll discuss this in more detail in the chapter on mutually beneficial data partnerships.

"Crosswalking" is the term we use to describe taking one dataset, like your CRM data, and using identifiable keys in the data to then match them against other databases. In this way, you can take the weather data tied to a particular zip code in a weather data file and *crosswalk* to your CRM file where your customer's zip codes are all stored. This gives you a picture of what the weather was and is like in their neighborhood on any given day. As we explore data appends and the process of crosswalking from one dataset to another, always consider how data privacy regulations require very specific contracts and terms regarding consent and removal of data.

So while you should definitely explore these data partnership types, you must also think about how the data will be used. In a humanized

---

6   "Pitney Bowes? Don't they just make stamp machines and postage meters?" They
     sure do. And each machine provides PB with an accurate location of the business
     that bought it and the businesses to whom the mail is sent. That's why their
     website header says "the simplest way to get the freshest data" and not "we make
     stamp machines."

approach, you must understand the act of improving your own data quality about your customers in relationship to those same customers' rights to understand the data you have about them and to request changes to or deletion of the data. In a dehumanized approach, the data about your customers can be highly valuable for you to leverage by crosswalking it into new contexts for new audiences that may also be interested in your services. This approach doesn't focus on these records as human beings, but more as raw data needing refinement and expansion. We pass no judgment on either approach, but you should understand how data appends and third-party processing partnerships differ in their approach.

Free Scans and Reports

What's my credit score? What is my business worth? What is the price of my home? How does my outfit look?[7] Every one of these questions is asked, routinely, online and in apps, and there are services that will do their best to answer them. The reality is that every online form, scan, report, or recommendation platform leverages a form of data partnership with the user. By entering information into the form, the user is providing the platform or report provider with the rights to the data submitted, and in many cases, this data partnership can be beneficial to both parties. Typically, the data transferred in these types of apps or scans are part of a dehumanized approach to data, because the usage rights granted to the company providing the free scan or free report tend to be very broad.

Take the credit score solutions as an example of this data partnership. Consumers seeking to access this data are significantly more likely to be contemplating a major life decision like marriage or, alternatively, a major purchase like a car or a home. When viewed from a humanized perspective, there are very few data points as personal and human as the timing around life decisions like these. To marketers, financial planners, insurance companies, and dozens of other business types, this signal is incredibly valuable, and when a consumer requests this data from the report provider, they are granting access to this life-changing intent. The provider of the scan or report can sell or share that data to any number of

---

7   Marvelous.

interested third parties because of the dehumanized approach. However, if the provider of the scan or service does not share the data, but rather uses it to specifically and only create a deeper relationship with the data subject, this could be the start of a truly humanized approach to servicing this customer. Once again, it is not necessarily the dataset itself but the business model and personal needs of the data company and individual data subjects that determine whether the company chooses a humanized or dehumanized approach.

But What Data Counts, Anyway?

If you look at both your current data assets and other data assets like those discussed above, you will identify unique circumstances related to your operations and use cases. In fact, it can be difficult, given the sheer volume of data, to know which data assets really matter or count. The unique collection of data assets for every business presents an interesting problem for those trying to find a way to identify meaningful, valuable data within the noise of daily business operations. For example, social media is a fascinating topic when it comes to GDPR compliance, because our nonstop tweets, snaps, pins, and bucket challenge videos gone awry generate an enormous amount of personal data that lives in the public sphere, effectively forever. Each piece of information constitutes a small part of the mosaic comprising our digital presence, and all of it can be analyzed, bundled, or sold. But, the question is, does this type of data even matter or count as personal data when it comes to privacy regulations?

Laws in the United States are notably narrow in their definition of what constitutes personal information. In Florida, for instance, the data breach notification law only applies when the data access includes a person's first name, last name, and another crucial piece of information, such as a Social Security number, credit card number, health insurance policy number, or email address and password. In other words, unless the breach involves the "crown jewels" of personal information, there's no obligation to report, because the rest of the data is not protected.

Not under the GDPR. Remember, the GDPR is all about the humanized approach.

The concept of personal data is far broader under the GDPR, and it is about much more than email passwords or credit card numbers. Every piece of data that does identify or could identify a person is "personal data" under the GDPR. That means traditional information like names, email accounts, and tax ID numbers are certainly personal data. But it also means everything from an IP address to a Facebook photo is as well.

This is a distinction with a difference, especially when it comes to companies unwittingly becoming subject to the GDPR. A company that markets and sells its goods in the United States and Italy, for instance, cannot use the same methods for all of its customers unless the methods are GDPR compliant. And a data breach at a US company that processes data on Floridians and Belgians may have no duty to notify the Florida Department of Legal Affairs, but may need to notify the Belgian Data Protection Authority within 72 hours.

Of course, one method to avoid an unnecessarily complicated data security policy is to simply create a GDPR-compliant privacy approach for your entire company, without regard to the origin of the data. But to the extent that is neither practicable nor economical, you need to have a firm grasp over what data you have, and whether it constitutes personal data under the regulation. At the same time, think now about how to create data security policies that emphasize security at every stage (as we describe in part IV), and remember that if you don't need the data, don't keep it. The GDPR may be complicated, but it isn't impossible to understand if you keep these principles in mind.

Data Minimization

Another principle worth considering is that data is not permanent unless we decide to make it so. We're accustomed to the view that, once your company secures information, it should hold onto it forever. Treating the information your company gathers in the same way you'd see on an episode of *Hoarders* is a dangerous approach, but a common one. Businesses amass a huge amount of information, much of it irrelevant or of marginal use, but they keep it just because it seems like it might be easier than deleting. They have also been taught for years in the United States that data gathered today may someday be useful in the future. This is an understandable but dangerous viewpoint because inadvertent data hoarding puts you at odds with one of the key principles of the GDPR: data minimization.

Minimization is the concept that a data controller should keep only the amount of data necessary to accomplish its ends, and not compile a portfolio of extraneous information on customers or clients. For the EU, this is about the citizen's fundamental right to privacy, preventing too much of their personal information from being held by those who do not need it. Under the GDPR, the less a company needs to know, the less it must collect. Therefore, asking for personal address details prior to shipping goods to a customer makes sense, but asking for their marital status probably does not.

If that seems like an outlier example, it shouldn't. There are countless examples of entities accumulating huge stores of information not directly tied to the good or service they provide to customers. Consider a company that requires website users to include confidential information to verify identity — mother's maiden name, for instance, which is a favorite target for identity thieves. If the company is hacked, even if the customer has closed their account, the risks are substantially higher for all involved than if the company had deleted the information when it was no longer necessary. For the same reasons, the company could have, and maybe should have, deleted the customer's home address and phone number. Minimizing the data you possess decreases the risk of harm if it is stolen.

There are other ways to minimize data, ranging from creating pseudonyms for customers ("pseudonymization"), to encryption, to "fading," where details of an account are gradually scrubbed over time. For instance, if a company once held a customer's email address, home address, phone number, and credit card information, they could delete the credit card information after a week or two, the phone number after a few more weeks, the home address after a few months, and eventually even the email address and name after sufficient time has passed. Fading keeps a customer's crucial information available only as long as it is necessary and deletes it when it is not. Email service providers, or ESPs, have long promoted the process of fading email addresses to ensure that you send emails only to those users who engage (even minimally) with prior attempts to reach them. On the other hand, if the customer has made no purchases in seven years and never opens your marketing or newsletter emails, why keep their email address, name, and credit card number any longer? Much of that information is likely out of date anyway.

The bottom line is that data minimization makes sense for all involved. It protects the customer's data and lowers the risk of harm to the company in the event of a breach. None of this is to say that companies should scrub all of their data too aggressively; indeed, data may be extremely valuable and a crucial component of a data sharing partnership. Instead, the point is to carefully analyze the data you possess, why you possess it, and what you're really doing with it. No CEO wants to find out that there was a data breach and that there wasn't any good reason for the company to have kept the sensitive data that was stolen.

So look through the data you have, catalog it, and decide whether it is valuable enough to keep, especially if it was created for a now-defunct data partnership. If you don't need the data for a partnership, and you don't need it for your own operations, do you really need it at all? You may conclude that the answer is yes and keep the data, but at least you will have done so after giving the subject real thought, and not simply because of "business-as-usual" inertia.

Beginning the DataSmart Method

These different perspectives of data (humanized and dehumanized), and the different approaches to management, security, and risks are all central components of the DataSmart Method. By breaking down every data strategy into a repeatable framework, our approach can be flexible enough to work in any market or regulatory environment.

We will describe the key steps in the methodology — *Identify*, *Value*, *Structure*, and *Protect* — in the following chapters. As we dive into each step in the method, remember that neither the fully dehumanized approach nor the humanized approach is appropriate, or even easy to define, in all situations. Maintaining this framework will ensure that, as the regulatory and technological tides shift, you can confidently build a data strategy that is adaptive and resilient.

Intrinsic Data

FINDING AND CREATING GREAT data partnerships starts with knowing what data you have. Step one is to identify every data asset within your organization. This not only is the basis for any data partnership strategy, it is also the only way to identify datasets that have regulatory and privacy issues. No matter what your role is at your company, you won't know all the data you have and produce until you go through this process. Identification is the first and most important step in the DataSmart Method.

You should consider two types of data: intrinsic data and extrinsic data. Intrinsic data is the data that your company creates, while extrinsic data is data about your company that other sources create. In this chapter, we address intrinsic data.

Intrinsic data exists because your business has come into existence or continues to operate. You and your employees typically gather, input, store, and maintain this data.

Extrinsic data, by contrast, is the far larger body of information created about, around, or tangential to your business. We will discuss extrinsic data in the next chapter.

The distinction between intrinsic and extrinsic data is important because of the difference in how ownership rights and derivative use cases apply to each. From the legal perspective, there are substantial differences in how to classify and protect intrinsic as opposed to extrinsic data, particularly when it comes to safeguarding consumer personal information and trade secrets.

fying Intrinsic Data Assets

It's best to identify data assets in stages. We prefer to start with a large whiteboard and continue with mind mapping software or a spreadsheet to document data types, field types, field characteristics, and notes on use and rights. If you approach this exercise with the right attitude, it can be an illuminating and a creative exercise, rather than an overwhelming chore. You can also begin to build team consensus and involvement in your data strategy by including representatives from different divisions of your company. An invaluable software program in this pursuit is iThoughtsHD. This software easily produced some of the mind map diagrams included in this book, and it synchronizes to the cloud for easy collaboration across teams.

Take a collaborative approach to identifying data assets across your organization. For example, many executives are unaware of what intrinsic data is created or tracked in all the various systems across their organization. By collaborating with different team members and inviting them to the whiteboard sessions, companies can gather the widest amount of input during the data identification process. The team you assemble for these exercises should be thought of as a "data strategy working group," and their involvement will ensure that multiple voices and perspectives are part of the process.

This is also a great opportunity to think creatively about how you can integrate privacy safeguards across platforms and datasets. It may not occur to you to institute a particular kind of precaution (say, role-based access controls, or RBACs) on a dataset unless you hear it mentioned in relation to another dataset. The data inventory is a critical part of your overall data security and compliance structure, too. Data security specialists will tell you that it is virtually impossible to protect your information if you don't have a complete understanding of what you have. You also can't fully understand your obligations to comply with the law if you don't know what law applies to each of those data assets.

For instance, online vendors routinely underestimate the scope of the information they collect and process. We constantly hear comments like, "We just sell widgets online. We don't have much beyond credit card numbers, and we're PCI compliant anyway."[8] Perhaps. But perhaps you are unaware of the extent to which your sales are, inadvertently, made to those under the age of 13, and as a result you may be subject to the Children's Online Privacy Protection Act (COPPA), which has a parental consent requirement. Or perhaps you don't realize that by advertising and selling in Belgium, you are subject to the GDPR, with its substantial requirements for processing and use limitation and its finicky rules on tracking cookies. The legal regimes that govern data, its processing, and its transfer are far more complicated than virtually anyone knows. Even lawyers don't usually realize how intricate the rules are.

The first step, then, is to understand the data you have so that you can make thoughtful, informed choices about how to protect it and how to use it. You need data security specialists and lawyers to review that inventory and help you identify where you may be subject to special requirements, and whether the general rules that apply to everyone have a particular wrinkle in your case.

With those thoughts in mind, let's start by examining where your intrinsic data mind map might start. We've prepared an example to give you a starting point (see Figure 1).

For many companies, this kind of simple, broad-stroke, mind map is the best place to begin. Each industry and corporate structure typically has the same first-level nodes, even if there are nuances regarding the depth of data under each node. For example, while a consumer products company will have sizable datasets about manufacturing, product, inventory, and transactional datasets, this doesn't mean they won't also have plenty of data stored under legal or compliance.

We recommend inviting members or individual leaders from each of the business groups shown in Figure 1 to join the data strategy working group, help identify data assets in this framework, and then build out from there. Often, individuals have a depth of knowledge about overlapping

---

8   PCI security standards are the technical and operational requirements for organizations accepting or processing payment transactions, and for software developers and manufacturers of applications and devices used in those transactions. If you process credit card transactions, you have to be PCI compliant.

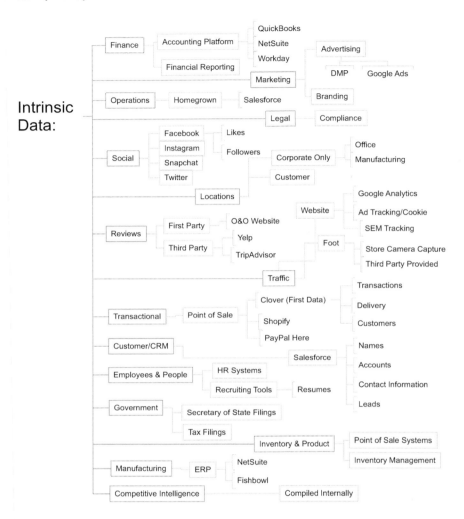

Figure 1: Sample Mind Map of Intrinsic Data Assets

areas. Starting at the node-one level, you should dig into each one of these centers with people that have intimate knowledge of the company's daily experience. In the rest of this chapter, we'll describe several of these intrinsic data categories in more detail.

Remember that this is actually a creative endeavor. Your goal is not to merely catalog and continue; that would be tedium. See this as both the catalog of the obvious and the revealing of hidden potential.

Financial Data

The most obvious and immediate data created by a business is its financial data. The company creates data about revenue and expenses in the normal course of operations, starting from day one.

The sheer volume of accounting and financial data created by a company is staggering, even for small businesses. Starting with the expenses side of the business, companies make a series of payments over time to vendors, employees, government entities, and a host of other parties to ensure they can operate efficiently. Viewed in monthly or quarterly reports of a few pages or tables, this dataset doesn't appear particularly robust. But that limited snapshot is deceptive, as the scope of detailed financial data over time is actually incredible. Financial data attracts data partners precisely because there is so much of it, and because it allows your partners to analyze it to understand consumer behavior or industry trends. You can monetize that kind of information quickly and consistently.

To understand why, start with vendor payments and which vendors are paid what amounts over time. What does the organization spend on building products, supplying services, and compensating outside parties? Analyzing shifts in the amount of money spent over time can create a consistent dataset that shows the variation in working with one vendor or contractor versus others. Data aggregation companies want this data so that they can forecast where dollars are being spent in an aggregate or industry-wide focus, and they will partner to receive this data in exchange for other datasets.

On the revenue side, who pays a company (and when) represents a huge dataset. We'll go into more detail on customer data later in this chapter, but beyond the list of customers, the timing of payments, sales, and their amounts become significantly valuable data assets over time. The transactions themselves are a microcosm of your business data; you can leverage the general revenue and income stream, even on a daily basis, to partner with those seeking to understand the flow of funds between business entities.

Consider the service provided by Philadelphia-based BizEquity.[9] This company provides a free business valuation service that bases estimates on revenue, expenses, and other basic financial data that the business owner enters into BizEquity's platform. BizEquity's proprietary valuation algorithm provides a company with a range of potential values for its entire business, should the owner want to sell or liquidate. Business owners, financial advisors, and legal and accounting professionals use these sophisticated and well-documented valuations every day to ensure that a business being valued is properly managed. This is an example of using the common, everyday exhaust of financial data from a business to produce an additional good of value.

While financial data is often treated as confidential (and for good reason), once you have identified how much of this data you have available historically, you can determine whether it can feasibly be of meaningful partnership value to others. By sharing some of your data in a humanized approach, without disclosing or sharing personal information about customers, you can help create new helpful datasets. To illustrate this point, ask yourself whether your business could benefit from an empirical, raw-data-based analysis of the primary financial trends in your industry, such as revenue growth for mid-cap companies located primarily in the southeastern United States. The answer is unquestionably yes: understanding those trends, especially at such a granular level, offers you insight that would otherwise be totally unavailable. Your partner, in return, is able to aggregate, market, and sell that same data across your industry, including to potential investors looking for opportunity. It's a relationship that offers clear, definable benefits to both sides.

Financial data is treated as confidential because it is archetypically sensitive and subject to a raft of regulations and laws (GLBA first springs to mind, but SEC and FINRA guidance on cybersecurity are also relevant). Personal financial information (PFI) is routinely the subject of state

---

9   Full disclosure: we work with BizEquity and provide them with data partnership/
     data privacy consulting.

data-breach notification requirements, and in some circumstances, companies are precluded from transferring financial data about their clients to non-affiliated entities. What is allowed depends on scope, purpose, and industry. Evaluating the potential regulations that would apply reinforces the critical value of identifying your data assets and their sensitivity.

Marketing Data from Advertising and Branding

Few people realize just how much data their marketing departments create and consume. The meteoric rise of the CMO as a data wizard in the last decade shows no signs of slowing, largely because the ever-growing list of digital marketing technology solutions enable the measurement of every penny spent, every keyword bid on, every billboard bought, and the traffic and ROI of all of these efforts. Why would any of this be valuable to a data partner? Aside from the mantra-like statement that "all data is valuable to someone,"[10] marketing data is useful because it shows your partner what *you* think is going to attract consumers. That kind of information, both on its own and in the aggregate, helps other marketers, advertisers, and content providers analyze their own approach to market targeting. You may use a digital marketing platform like Marketo, Infusionsoft, or HubSpot to track your digital marketing and ROI. If so, from the data intrinsically produced by your marketing activities, you agree to grant that same platform the right to use your data in exchange for providing you with industry trends and aggregated insights about what tactics other companies are using. The digital marketing platform can then sell this usage data to other specialized digital marketing companies that will build new apps and products that integrate directly into the same digital marketing platform. You could then buy this new add-on service, thus sharing more data back with your digital marketing platform.[11]

---

10   As well as being mantra-like, this statement has the added benefit of being true. Marketing analytics on ROI and click-throughs are a major component of many marketing companies' business plan.

11   This is where we start singing "Circle of Life" from *The Lion King*.

There is data created specifically by your business to attract customers, beginning with the advertising copy, images, content, and facts about your business that you present to the world. Consider television and radio spots, when they air, what content they include, and how much they cost. Then gather all of your digital marketing expenditure across platforms like Google Ads, Facebook, Twitter, Snapchat, and Instagram. Gather the keywords, bid data, content, and word choices of all of these advertisements and promotions. Any advertising expenditure, in any form, should be relatively easy to identify. Depending on the retention savvy of your marketing team, much of this data is available already and logged over time in a form that would be potentially valuable to partners.

Branding is also a key dataset to gather. In the next chapter, we will discuss all the content created around or about your brand (not by your own doing), but for now, focus on the intrinsic data assets. This will include logos, website content, blog posts, and anything else that your marketing team uses in its effort to manage the messaging and perception of the company through brand.

Large portions of this data may also be available from your digital agency, if you employ one. Companies with digital agencies often end up with multiple campaign strategies leveraging brand assets and content across a wide variety of platforms aimed at different audiences. Because digital agencies constantly have to demonstrate their ongoing value to your business, they usually maintain a comprehensive dataset of what messaging was bought or pushed where and when. This helps them demonstrate impact and, ultimately, marketing and branding ROI. Tap this data repository in the process of identifying your intrinsic brand assets.

Transactional Data

Depending on the industry, transactional data can be one of the most beneficial datasets to compile and store over time. Any business with a point of sale system, or POS, will easily have access to this dataset, which will highlight what products or goods were sold, when, and sometimes, to whom. Capturing whom a business sells their products or services to is, unfortunately, not automatic, so you must consciously build it into many POS workflows, as we discuss below.

Transactions, from the single-cash-register business to the multinational consumer goods discount retailer, are a fantastic source of data partnership raw material. Knowing what products or services are selling at scale, where, and when drives the underpinnings of any economy. Further, when this data is analyzed along with financial data around what vendors are being paid for materials, investors and economists can start to build a phenomenal model of supply and demand. For this reason, data partnerships and distribution deals have long sought transactional data, which creates an obvious opportunity for you to get the most value from your data assets.

For companies that focus on product sales, rather than services or appointments, the POS system will log each item sold, at what price, the inventory status, and dozens of other data fields. These often include which department the item was sold from, what location made the sale, which salesperson recorded it, and even what discounts or specials were applied to the sale. It's a robust dataset. POS platforms like Square, Clover, or Micros will provide you with an automated way of aggregating and storing this data, typically including excellent insight reporting.

For service companies, or those that schedule appointments and provide service on-site or at a specific location, there are additional tools that can help you gather data. Most POS platforms for these cases include the concepts of scheduling and availability. For example, these platforms will be loaded with the number of available stylists at a hair salon along with their schedule of available times. This is then combined with product purchase data, tracking when a customer purchases hair care products shortly after receiving a haircut. Firms like MINDBODY are at the forefront of scheduling software that incorporates all POS and transactional functionality.

Remember, significant amounts of this transaction data can relate to people and contain personal information. As you build your data library, tracking the available fields and content of your transaction data, you should document which fields and which systems contain personal data. Many businesses have changed their transactional systems of record several times in their history, making tracking more difficult. In these cases, you need to know both where the transactional data is and where it was in the past.

Customer and CRM Data

Customer contact information is one of the most important and sacred types of data assets. Who buys from you and how you retain those relationships and eventually grow them is at the heart of every customer relationship management platform. While this data is very valuable, many businesses do a poor job of keeping it fresh and up to date, which leads to a decay in the value of the asset. Because someone who purchased three years ago from a local business may no longer even live in the area, keeping CRM data records correct and updated is a primary task associated with customer data.

Capturing customer data seems an obvious necessity, but it is striking how many businesses we have seen that don't take a proactive approach to CRM integration into their work process. Every major company or organization needs to create a culture of customer and prospect data capture throughout their enterprise. Many platforms like Salesforce.com specifically provide tools for this capture, but it fundamentally comes down to forcing your teams to recognize that gathering customer data points is essential to their own success, as well as the company's. We've seen and worked with plenty of organizations that mandate complete data-field fill rates in order for a salesperson or account manager to be eligible for a commission on a sale, which, needless to say, essentially guarantees compliance.

CRM dataset upkeep can generate enormous amounts of wasted effort in data creation and collection because many of the fields gathered are already available from other sources. There are many platforms that will append their own or other datasets to your CRM data to create a more robust view of your customers and prospects. We will discuss this type of enhancement in the next chapter, but the important thing is that CRM and customer data should focus on the unique attributes that your business creates. What the customer purchased from your company, when, at what price, and from whom are intrinsic data points unique to your business, existing only because of your interactions with the customer.

The customer's address, company, place of business, interests, hobbies, and even their phone number can all be easily appended later through any number of data enhancement platforms. The email address of the customer is the most important factor typically used to crosswalk across datasets (as we described in the last chapter) and should always be a mandatory CRM field.

Minimizing friction in the gathering of customer data is very important when it comes to keeping both your customer and your employees sane. However, there are many regulations, including the GDPR, that also want you to think of the data you have about or around individuals in a new, more minimalistic way. Having countless additional data fields on old records about people is relatively worthless to your enterprise, but creates a potential liability based upon these new privacy regulations. For this reason, when you review your CRM assets and identify them, this is an excellent time to consult with your data protection officer (DPO) or counsel to ensure you are building data privacy into your systems by design.

Your CRM data is among the most important to consider when it comes to implementing a security and privacy regime. For the most part, data security and privacy regulations treat consumer data as the most important because it relates to actual, identifiable people. That's true regardless of where you operate — the Federal Trade Commission (FTC) in the United States treats consumer protection as one of its primary aims, and the EU's GDPR is specifically aimed at protecting the personal data of European citizens. When you analyze your customer-related intrinsic data, you need to ensure that your inventory is taking place in a secure environment, with meaningful safeguards in place. For instance, restrict access to your CRM to only those personnel who are trained to protect the information. Keeping things "need-to-know" can help ensure that your customers' data remains safe, and you remain out of the crosshairs of privacy regulators.

Employee and People Data

Companies often overlook employee data as a source of useful information, treating it as useful merely for internal operations. That's a mistake.

Not only does employee data represent a warehouse of reviewable data about your workforce and their capabilities and backgrounds, it also offers insight into their performance over time, their response to company initiatives and plans, and the relationship between their efforts and company success. In fact, some of the most exciting advances in data analysis focus on employee information, providing management and staff with helpful tools to evaluate success and performance metrics.

Among the many forms and data points generated through the employee hiring process, résumés stand out for their personal and business information. Platforms like ZipRecruiter.com enable candidates and recruiters to gather data about your business by providing insights or data about candidates, application trends, and your own hiring metrics. Where potential employees worked previously, their roles, their projects, and their accomplishments are all important datasets to understand and document. You should treat this personal information with a guarded, humanized approach, but also analyze it in relationship to your business. What types of people apply for roles at your company and why?

From an operations standpoint, the intrinsic data created by employees — like work schedules, access times, efficiency, sales velocity, customer feedback and a host of other metrics — are central to ensuring an efficient operation. You should also apply that data later for compensation reviews. Data is crucial in problematic employee situations where a company needs to defend itself with facts about an employee's actions, or inaction, within the workplace. If you don't have a plan to identify this data, you will have difficulty accessing it later, when you need it.

You can also gather data directly from employees. Using local information, feedback, and polls, businesses are tapping employees to help create data beyond their normal work duties. For example, several data companies pay employees to check and confirm local data when they travel or go on vacation to locations around the globe. In exchange for payments that cover gas or a couple of meals per day on a trip, the company asks only that the employee verify information about local businesses as part of their journey. It's an intelligent way to further leverage your workforce to increase your data assets or to verify data you already possess.

Operations Data

The operations of a business, outside of the transactional and financial, typically include information about offices, locations, infrastructure, utilities, software licenses, security access, and broader vendor relationships. Most businesses have an officer or executive head of operations with a broad view that touches on more areas of the business than other executives. Because of this access, it makes sense to include the chief operating officer, or members of their organization, in any data identification exercise.

Operational data will center around key performance indicators, or KPIs, because they measure the operational efficiency of the business at any given time. Because of this, the operations team often receives significant amounts of data from the other divisions of a company for aggregation and analysis, further increasing this team's ability to identify intrinsic data assets.

Some of the most valuable operations-related intrinsic datasets focus on the efficiency of a business, including its customer experience, support, and turnover. Most companies now have a customer success team focused on ensuring that each customer has a quality product or service experience. The operations group often manages the teams responsible for this effort because it also manages the delivery and follow-up with the business's customers. For example, the operations teams at FedEx or UPS track every package, its delivery, and the feedback from customers the world over. Operations data often overlaps with transactional and financial data, but the operations team manages the actual execution of the product or service and the feedback loop from the customer.

Partnerships around these datasets are growing. Companies like Zendesk that track every customer complaint, praise point, or question produce enormous amounts of data with both business and personal information attached. Operations teams manage this information, respond to it, and quickly amass guides, frameworks, and response protocols to handle each type of customer interaction, from the happiest fanatic to the angriest detractor. By identifying the data types, amounts, and privacy constraints in your operations group, you will locate the data that is needed for industry-wide understanding of typical operational efficiencies.

Legal and Compliance Data

Legal and compliance departments generate data on a surprising scale. Lawyers create multiple iterations of documents that reflect the input of various interested parties, and keep each of the versions of the document stored so that they can later determine who wanted what and why. Compliance officers have to create massive files for submission to regulators. Ask the compliance team of a publicly traded company how many forests were cut down to file last year's SEC and Sarbanes-Oxley reports, and they'll wince. Responding to a subpoena or civil investigative demand also creates a massive amount of data, much of it highly sensitive and privileged. The three categories we've just described easily take up terabytes of memory and they're not even substantive data about your operations. They're just the data about your data.[12]

There are also tracking and ongoing compliance efforts. Companies with enterprise-scale compliance systems have an approval workflow that maintains dates, time, and approvals or rejections about any decision in the chain. That information has less intrinsic value than, for instance, a customer list or account number, but under the right circumstances, a complete record of transactions, authorizations, and decision-makers can be the difference between success and failure in the courtroom, or between a simple filing with a regulator and a protracted, costly, reputation-damaging investigation.

Government-Related Data

Regardless of the industry, every business operating requires some interaction with the government, including its articles of incorporation or creation and its quarterly and annual financial statements for tax purposes. The government compiles data about every business and utilizes this information in economic forecasting as well as for its own budgetary process.

---

12   Not to be confused with metadata, which is something lawyers have finally learned about and now think they understand. They don't.

For most businesses, a combination of corporate finance and corporate counsel staffs work together to create the data and information to provide to each appropriate government entity. Additionally, businesses that operate directly with or provide services to the government must subject themselves to additional data requests including background information and detailed operating statements. The government requires strict adherence to reporting requirements; however, many businesses use outsourced agents to deal with government mandates for reporting.

Product and Inventory Data

Product data is perhaps one of the most robust datasets that any company or business will generate. This data is created by the company, or, in the case of distribution or retail sales, is created by another firm and then entered into the company's inventory and product platforms. In either case, the amount of information about a given product is substantial. One need only look at the web code on a typical retail product page online, whether on the Walmart, Home Depot, or Amazon site, to see the depth of variables about every product.

This data may include measurements, color, creation date, weight, style, quantity, safety regulations, details, description, instructions, electrical requirements, expiration dates, delivery, and dozens of additional data fields. These product data points vary greatly by specific industry and product type, but are growing in every industry. The amount of content available about the tires on a car is as varied as the data about the car itself. For this reason, you need to manage product data and lists in data platforms specifically designed for the appropriate dataset. The auto industry is a great example of this, with inventory systems that surround and connect the product data into a tightly woven ecosystem. This connection between product and inventory, or the availability of a particular product at a particular location or time, creates highly customized datasets for your business.

One other note about products and inventories: remember that you don't have to sell products to have inventory. Most service-based businesses have an inventory of available services. The number of open tables and seats at a restaurant at a given time is its inventory of available capacity, which renews as customers finish their meals and leave and the table is "turned" by the staff to be ready for the next guest to use. This is a time-sensitive inventory, tied to the consumption of food and beverage items that have their own product schema. Restaurants mix inventory of availability with availability of menu and drink items, creating a very complex dataset. Think of all the datasets produced by a popular restaurant on a busy night. Menus, selections, payments, guests, reservations, table availability, reviews, inventory, allergen lists, beverages, sales, employee schedules; all are produced and reproduced each day the restaurant is open.

Published Content Data

While content is a very broad term, we focus here on original content that your business produces. Whether you're publishing a blog, news article, song review, video announcement, podcast, or any number of other content types, the data both inside and around this content is intrinsic data produced by your business. For media companies, the content they produce is essentially their product with its own metadata including publisher data, topics, keywords, titles, authors, sources, categories, publication dates, and hundreds of other attributes.

In addition to this data about the content, there is significant data to be found inside the content itself. Using natural language processing (NLP) tools,[13] content with written or spoken words can be analyzed to extract topics, entities, companies, people, trends, and even tone. Platforms like Amazon Lex, IBM Watson, Google Cloud Natural Language, and Thomson Reuters Open Calais provide NLP as a service, enabling content producers to extract these facts and data assets from the content they produce.

Content data is also the critical ingredient in search discovery. The content on webpages or published sites drives the most significant understanding of a site's purpose or value and is the basis for search engine

---

13 "In Depth Guide for Natural Language Platforms," AppliedAI, April 9, 2018, https://blog.appliedai.com/natural-language-platforms/.

optimization (SEO) strategies. Of course, inbound links to your content have always been the biggest driver of search rank, but what gets those inbound links is the efficient discovery by others of the excellent content you produce. The data you produce and make easily accessible with your content is an important intrinsic dataset to document in the identification process.

In addition to the data about your content, there is traffic and search data that relates to every piece of content you produce. Typically, traffic is an extrinsic dataset because it is created by others; however, the storage and attribution of your traffic as it relates to your content is very important and should be documented with your content. This is important to gain an understanding both of your content's appeal and of your audience and its content preferences. Tracking of content readership, sharing, and audience interaction is the basis of platforms like Google Analytics, Parse.ly, and Searchmetrics. These platforms will provide detailed data about your content, and although it is created by others through their interaction with your content, you should consider these metrics as intrinsic to your content data.

Manufacturing Data

For businesses that manufacture goods and products, the supply side of the process as well as the timing of the creation of those goods and products creates intrinsic datasets. If your business manufactures items for sale or distribution, then the vendors, payments, purchase orders, ingredients, and dozens of data points in your purchasing process are highly specific to your business. Plenty of data companies only focus upon analyzing where and when manufacturing companies purchase new equipment to meet their production goals. In fact, some companies, like Apple, go to enormous efforts to protect their manufacturing data and vendors, treating their supply-chain dealings as confidential trade secrets.

Another primary dataset in manufacturing is the production times and delivery times of the items being produced. Countless models and economic analyses are focused on manufacturing capacity and delivery speed. These metrics of operational efficiency can be broken down by individual manufactured item to provide additional insight. For example, the creation, manufacturing, and delivery of a Honda SUV may be substantially different from that of a Honda motorcycle, and each process, including its dates, is important to record.

Intrinsic data about manufacturing and delivery of goods is also expanding rapidly due to the advent of the Internet of Things (IoT) sensor boom. Warehouses, production facilities, and delivery vehicles are all now producing data of their own to track the progress of one box of goods or another from creation to distribution. Consider IoT sensors that track agriculture products, their harvest dates, times, humidity levels, and temperatures to ensure that a shipment of lettuce doesn't sit in a truck for too long at too high or too low of a temperature. These sensors report back the data to central processing stations where the tracking GPS signals notify managers of the location and time of each situation. This type of intrinsically created data is scaling rapidly and will likely overtake many other forms of intrinsic data in terms of quantity.

Location Data

Many businesses operate out of specific locations or service areas. The data surrounding these locations are one of their intrinsic datasets. This data includes hours of operation, products available, staff present, menu, events, customer base serviced, reviews, and more. At first glance, you may not recognize the enormous amount of custom information that your business has in this space.

Location data plays an overt role in customer discovery as almost every search for a business, product, or service is, at least initially, confined to "nearby" or "near me." In fact, Google and other search engines apply a "nearby" filter to your searches even if you don't actually type in the word itself. This is because location data drives the proximity and time to purchase, which in turn drives value to your business. For many businesses, partnering with a platform like Yext,[14] which is designed to provide knowledge management around data types like businesses location, is a helpful first step in identifying these data assets.

---

14   Full disclosure: Christian formerly worked at Yext.

Social Network Data

Social sites like Facebook, Instagram, Snapchat, Twitter, and LinkedIn have substantial data assets created by your business. While we will look at this same group of data sites from the extrinsic perspective in the next chapter, they are also a source of intrinsic data.

Depending upon the size of your enterprise, there are likely several people involved in social media promotion and response at your firm. Creating, posting, sharing, liking, responding, and commenting are excellent ways to create a dataset that shows, in parallel to your transactions, an ongoing dialogue with the customer or community that surrounds your business. You should store every correspondence, post, and comment as you begin to analyze the value of data created by your company. In many instances, the influence of a particular company and their operations may far exceed their actual operation, which can, in turn, increase the value of their data. In all too many cases, companies do not store this social data centrally, as different departments, teams, and even executives post and respond directly; this creates a highly fragmented approach.

Social data also plays an important role in discovery and the search ecosystem. Search engine optimization is moving from a Google-centric, search box focused process to one that also includes searches by voice. Like the review content we describe below, social content created by your business is part of this optimization, and will play a more important role in the discovery of your business going forward. The content you create, share, and engage with as a company will be visible to would-be customers in response to visual and voice prompts. By identifying where and how you are creating this content across your company, you are better prepared to deal with the increasing role of social content.

Review-Related Data

Reviews about a company, its business, locations, products, employees, and services have skyrocketed over the last decade as more platforms create spaces where these reviews can be posted. Reviews are typically extrinsic data created about or around a business, which we will cover in more depth in the next chapter. However, the business itself typically creates the responses to these reviews along with other social content.

The dialogue between reviews, good or bad, and a business has become an essential success metric that goes well beyond good customer service and support. Depending on the size and complexity of the company, listening for review content and then routing, approving, and managing responses may require enterprise-grade software. The responses and approvals create timelines in data that can later be analyzed alongside other datasets to ensure the content is having the desired reaction. Like social media content, the content of reviews is often generated by a number of people at a business, but in recent years companies are taking a more coordinated approach. Learn from this trend: designate one person or team to be responsible for all monitoring and responses to reviews.

Companies also generate reviews by reaching out to customers and asking for them. This can be as simple as a message on the bottom of a printed receipt, or part of a complex email lifecycle marketing campaign across several touchpoints and triggers over the course of months. Companies like Yotpo, a commerce marketing platform in New York, combine social content, review generation, and transaction data to optimize the experience of the customer with the business. Regardless of the method, reviews generated through the normal course of business are a worthwhile dataset to store and keep with a proper date and time stamp.

Competitive Intelligence Data

Companies typically amass information about their competition. This research is best accomplished over time by storing data initially from the competitors' websites and marketing materials and then building upon that with spreadsheets, feature comparisons, client lists, and other tools. We recommend that you consider deploying dedicated resources to this effort, if you haven't already. From a data perspective, the beauty of the competitive tracking dataset is that it can highlight trends in the market and opportunities in adjacent markets that may not have initially appeared to your team, an effort that is also extremely valuable in identifying new data partners.

In our next chapter, we will discuss extrinsic competitive datasets that you can buy from third-party data providers who pull together data across a wide spectrum of disciplines, which you can then append to your own competitive data.

Summarizing Intrinsic Datasets

While the intrinsic datasets we've just described, created internally by your business, will vary depending upon the industry or specialty of your company, it is likely that you will have some data in each category.

When building out your asset library, remember that this effort starts with a collaborative effort across teams at your company. No single person is likely to have all the answers or even be aware of what every team has, unless you have already hired and empowered a chief data officer.

One other item to include in your analysis is a way to flag each data element as either confidential or personal data. We discuss what constitutes personal data given different regulatory frameworks and jurisdictions later in the book, but for the purposes of moving expeditiously through the identification process, you should be conservative in your approach and keep track of any data field that might contain personal data. If you believe that a data point may provide a key to unlock anonymized datasets, or identify a person, you should flag it for consideration and then work with counsel to categorize it at a later time. Because your goal is to identify as many data assets as it is possible to gather, don't exclude personally identifiable information (PII) or any other confidential dataset, such as contracts, from this process. Later, when we discuss how to leverage the value of your data assets through partnerships, we will share how to build structures and best practices that protect this type of information.

Now that you have the initial framework for identifying intrinsic data assets created by the existence of your business, it is time to broaden the scope of available data to include extrinsic data.

4

Extrinsic Data

EXTRINSIC DATA IS THE data created about or around your business by other people, machines, or platforms. For example, satellites map and photograph your store locations, autonomous mapping vehicles take photos of your storefront, customers snap poorly lit interior shots, reviewers ruthlessly hammer your cuisine, and financial analysts distribute reports predicting the imminent demise of your business. And that was all just in the last 15 minutes.

Extrinsic data is everywhere, and, from a scale perspective, it will dwarf your intrinsic datasets. Extrinsic data is the key to unlocking the leverage in your intrinsic data. As you build your data strategy, extrinsic data that somehow touches or is about your business will certainly help you identify the exact types of datasets you will partner with in the future.

One of the best ways to inform your data partnership approach is to understand the data assets that you create internally and their relationship to data assets created by third parties externally. If you focus solely internally, you won't be able to see all the external data suppliers who can generate the best value from your data.

Instead, focus system by system, examining each source of extrinsic data as an ecosystem related to your business. Then focus on which external companies specialize in the data for each ecosystem.

By understanding all of the different types of extrinsic data encircling your business, you will quickly see that partnerships with these companies can enhance your data and theirs.

Identifying Extrinsic Data

There are several steps in the process of identifying extrinsic data. While there are platforms that will help to "listen" for your company name, brands, products, and services, as well as those of your competitors, many of these platforms focus only on a few key areas like social media and news content. We recommend seeking a far broader sweep of datasets to incorporate into your analysis.

Gathering external datasets around your business adds detail, relationships, accuracy, and value to your internal data. To make them useful, you must connect them with a unique or key value that you already have in your dataset (product SKU, date and time stamps, or social media handles, for example) that allows you to match your intrinsic data to extrinsic datasets. These relationships between data entities demand a complex ecosystem design that allows you to crosswalk from one dataset to another. By connecting intrinsic and extrinsic datasets, you can significantly increase both the accuracy and the value of your data, and therefore help others extract more value from your data.

We have organized this chapter around the same sorts of categories of data as in the previous chapter, focusing this time on data available from external sources, rather than internally. In many cases, the platforms and companies that control these datasets sell them or license them, but those same platforms and companies may also share data with you freely in exchange for access and rights to use some of your data in return. One such example is the business scans and free analysis report business that we described earlier.

The easiest way to identify new potential extrinsic data partnerships is to start with the internal data you create and then see who uses that data in external products or services. Our goal is to highlight what kinds of relationships to look for, after which you can adjust your approach appropriately to find the right data partners to suit your needs.

While we will include many different data companies and potential partners for you to investigate in this section, this list is by no means exhaustive. Our goal here is to identify what types of assets are out there and give some representative examples. We have dealt directly with many of the businesses mentioned here and can testify to both their willingness to partner and their expertise in their respective datasets. Let's jump into identifying extrinsic data and look to uncover potential data partner counterparties.

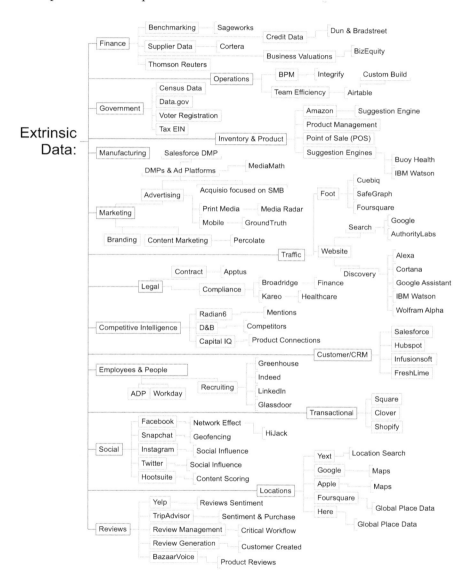

Figure 2: Sample Mind Map of Externally Created Data Assets

Financial Data

Your company's intrinsic financial data focuses upon the revenues and expenses your firm earns from or pays to over specific time periods. This information ultimately provides a helpful financial view of your business and its health and growth prospects. To extend this view to extrinsic financial data, start with industry benchmark data about similarly situated businesses.

Extrinsic financial data around your company include metrics like valuations, industry growth trends, supplier payments, economic growth, competitor insights, credit ratings, accounting standards, and debt analysis ratios.

Credit data has been one of the most important external datasets for decades. Platforms such as Dun & Bradstreet have been providing credit ratings for over 100 years. They have evolved into large data stores that present promising partnership opportunities. They focus not only on credit reporting and analysis, but on hundreds of fields of information about businesses like yours. D&B, Equifax, Experian, and similar firms have both consumer data and business data and provide reports, some of which are free, to enable businesses to understand their ratings. Generally, licensees pay D&B to augment data on businesses and customers, but D&B also seeks businesses to provide information directly to them so they can add to their repository and models.

Financial data is also useful for benchmarking and building industry-standard metrics. It takes an enormous amount of data to provide truly valuable metrics, from small businesses all the way up to enterprise-level financial data. Sage, based in Raleigh, North Carolina, has compiled this scale of data through many years of providing global accounting software solutions to small- and medium-sized businesses. Their platform feeds a massive proprietary database on risk, valuations, and other characteristics of private companies. Customers pay to use the Sage accounting software, while Sage gets some rights to aggregate anonymized accounting data to refine their models based on the ever-changing financial updates from customers. Once again, your partnership potential here really depends upon your business's own data assets, but those with substantial financial data, across many geographies and industries, could definitely benefit from the benchmarking insights of a firm like Sage.

Cortera, based in Boca Raton, Florida, is an innovative company in the field of credit and financial data. Cortera provides credit analysis and data about all forms of financial transactions, but its unique perspective comes from access to business-to-business transactions from millions of businesses. Cortera takes a very focused approach to the creditworthiness of businesses by analyzing the transactions between businesses, using data supplied by those businesses' customers. Cortera has data partnerships across dozens of industries, which reflects both their capabilities and their open partnership framework.

These are just a few examples of external financial datasets that are immediately available as potential partners. If your business can provide financial data to these companies as a customer or as a partner, you can gain rights to append or augment your data with their industry or competitive insight, helping benchmark your company's results and financial health. These companies seek your information to constantly improve their own data models and products, which leads to a highly mutually beneficial relationship.

Financial data is an excellent basis for finding and growing data partnerships because it is likely that your company would benefit from knowing benchmarks and levels for companies comparable to yours. Knowing what other businesses spend on marketing, sales, distribution, research, and all other aspects of their operations is helpful in managing your direction; a partnership with a third party that gathers this type of extrinsic data is the way to get there. This data can guide your own revenue and expenditure expectations.

Marketing and Advertising Data

As we explained in chapter 3, there is no shortage of data surrounding your business's marketing and advertising expenditures. The growth in data, analytics, dashboards, and insight providers has skyrocketed in the last decade. At this point, the CMO and their team at your company (and every other) likely have as many systems and data tools as your CTO or CIO. This growth in marketing data and tracking represents an ideal data store. With a virtually limitless set of marketing data partnership opportunities, your CMO, who will be familiar with the value in marketing and advertising data, will become an outstanding ally.

For example, digital advertising has evolved from the old world of web banner and display ads to fully integrated, real-time, bidding platforms, modeled after some of the most complex Wall Street trading algorithms, that allow you to maximize your marketing spend across hundreds of different sites and search platforms. This transformation continues to evolve with ever-increasing expenditure and the explosion of mobile advertising.

MediaMath, Salesforce DMP, and Acquisio are three outstanding data management platforms (DMPs) that allow you to manage digital purchasing and expenditure. Part of the appeal of a DMP is that it encompasses all of the data and purchasing activity across its user base to augment and improve the efficiency of its algorithms. The more businesses that use these platforms, the smarter they get. Part of their solution is gathering the keywords, sites, bid prices, long-tail targets, geographies, and timing distributions from their massive client bases. All of these platforms also have robust application programming interfaces (APIs)[15] and export features that allow you to analyze your expenditures, ROI, and timing to help you improve your own spend.

When it comes to print and broadcast media, or "old media," there are also some powerful external data sources. From magazines to television to radio, these media formats continue to command massive amounts of spend from businesses, likely yours included. One standout platform in this area is MediaRadar, based in Manhattan. This company originally built impressive scanning and optical character recognition platforms for magazines that scan every ad on every page in every issue and combine that data with the cost of those ads. This allowed its customers to know exactly what page 25 in *Vogue* magazine would cost to advertise upon, and, sometimes more importantly, how many ads by their competitors would

---

15   An API is the set of tools that facilitates communication between systems and servers, essentially allowing users to access and make use of information held in the platform.

precede and follow theirs in the same issue. MediaRadar has expanded substantially and now features an excellent data asset: a massive product and brand database, built almost by the exhaust of their scanning engine.

Mobile ad spending continues to spike, and there are dozens of excellent companies tackling this data-rich space. GroundTruth, based in New York City and formerly known as xAd, takes mobile and location advertising where everyone is dying to go, which is location targeting in real time. In other words, if you want to drop a lunchtime ad on every mobile phone within 500 yards of your restaurant location, GroundTruth can make that happen. Mobile advertising pulls in substantial additional data assets like business locations, store hours, physical footprint (or geofences), personal phone identifiers, cookies, and a large ad inventory through platforms. GroundTruth then combines all of these to deliver the most valuable mobile ad experience to its customers. As a result, its platform provides reporting capabilities that have enabled many other data businesses to sprout up around it, using its reporting APIs to create custom metrics about your business.

In addition to all of the ad-tech out there, most companies also want a powerful way to market their brand through the use of brand assets and content. This is a significant undertaking as global companies typically manage multiple brands, often across many different industries and use cases. For this reason, companies such as Percolate have built content management systems to help the CMO and their team to identify the company's content assets and manage their deployment. Percolate includes a feature that allows you to visualize this data through an intuitive calendar view that highlights all of the content, when it will be published, where, and through which medium. Marketers can then coordinate this calendar with ad spend to boost content and brand awareness. Because the goal is for consumers to see, interact with, and hopefully share or act upon this content, platforms like Percolate also provide data tracking and export functionality.

The value of an extrinsic data partnership in marketing is both knowledge and distribution or channel opportunities. Knowing the engagement that other companies are getting from the different potential marketing approaches they are taking is how marketers stay relevant in a constantly changing environment. Remember, marketers constantly destroy the capabilities to reach an audience by overuse and overreach. Direct mail, billboards, radio, television, email, text messaging, in-app notices... all of these ways to reach customers for a given product or tool tend to become saturated, and even regulated at some point. CAN-SPAM and Do Not Call regulations are examples of this pattern. A data partnership with companies that gather marketing efforts across industries and channels is the best way to gain access to volume metrics and trend, so that you can stay on the train or get off, rather than end up on the tracks.

Transactional Data

Finding the right data partner around transactional data can also help you build an effective channel strategy. If you generate significant transactional data and can identify a partner that aggregates this content in a meaningful way, that partner will reveal to you other symbiotic companies that may be ideal to distribute or market your product. In other words, if you sell a high volume of hats, and you provide the transactional data to a partner that aggregates head sizes, they are likely to know other companies that would like to sell your hats.

As discussed earlier, point of sale systems help manage the transactional data that your business creates. POS companies like Square, Clover, and Shopify take a product or service list, complete with all details, and make products on that list available for purchase through a connection to online ordering and credit card transactions on a kiosk or a tablet- or phone-based mobile payment app. This data is the lifeblood of retail sales and in-person shops and also drives online sales figures. Each transaction captures the product sold, the service bought, the date, time, seller, method of payment, amount of payment, and location of transaction, for example. From here, the POS platform stores the data and makes it available for export and analysis.

Most POS platforms are available in versions for vertical or industry-specific use. This means restaurant POS systems focus on menus and delivery while the dentist's office POS systems focus on insurance carriers, reimbursement codes, and common services. This specialization ensures that businesses no longer need to customize the software to their particular use case, and most are willing to pay a premium for POS software that is designed for their type of business.

Transactional data is undeniably valuable for your data partnership strategy. Through the normal course of business, you will be able to see and track trends in what is purchased, which can lead to insight beyond just your store or operation. For this reason, many transaction POS platforms market additional datasets like benchmarking, trend analysis, and competitor insights, which they may provide to you through a mutually beneficial partnership. There is hardly a business out there that doesn't want to know what comparable businesses are selling more and less of, and what the competition is up to. These POS platforms are able to break that data down by industry, geography, product, service, and even time of day. We have found that the data teams behind many POS platforms will engage with you to share or offer introductions to other potential partners that contribute data through their system.

Customer and CRM Data

Customer data is a critical factor in all data partnership strategies. However, you must understand limitations on partnering around customer data that includes personally identifiable information and is subject to regulatory and legal constraints. Additionally, most businesses view this information to be confidential and proprietary, so they must anonymize it before sharing it with partners.

The world leader in CRM is Salesforce.com. Salesforce has built not only one of the most robust and scalable platforms to manage CRM assets, but also an open framework to allow thousands of other companies to provide applications (or apps) to work securely with the data stored in the cloud. This walled garden has given many companies that seek to provide valuable customer analytics and tools the opportunity to build connected apps that augment the basic Salesforce.com solution.

Few app markets or integration libraries are as successful as Salesforce's. With so many integrations, the Salesforce AppExchange and Service Cloud concepts open up tremendous opportunities to share data, increase quality, and build upon customer data.

Many apps in the Salesforce AppExchange allow you to improve the data you have about your customers by appending additional data facts, models, or scores. Companies like Acxiom, Experian, and Clearbit provide these data append solutions, with customer data attributes that can help you communicate with and target the right segments of your audience.

Another common use case is to "clone" your customer dataset. This is done by selecting a subset of top customers and providing a file from your CRM, usually as an export, to a third-party customer modeling company. Firms such as Infogroup or Hoovers can then take those customers and their core attributes and run an analysis to find other customers similar to the those you already have. This process of cloning or finding similar potential customers can deliver excellent results, but its value depends on the quality of the modeling partners' data and efficacy of their models. The best way to attempt to work with any of these modeling partners is to request a test, where you are permitted to download, use, and analyze a subset of results.

One last, exciting area of development in CRM is the scoring, evaluation, and improvement of interactions with customers. While treating current customers well, ensuring they have an excellent experience, and striving to retain them as future customers drives higher lifetime value, the actual process of using data to achieve these goals is still relatively new territory. One company taking this to new levels is Gainsight, which analyzes every interaction with customers to ensure that a business maximizes its retention and growth. By integrating with Salesforce data, Gainsight models the customer touchpoints and success metrics that signal the health of each account. This integration then adds additional datasets that are proprietary to your company to increase the available insight.

Another company leveraging customer data and transactions is FreshLime. FreshLime is a start-up that takes transaction and financial data and marries it to customer or CRM data to provide lifecycle messaging and marketing. While the world spends countless dollars to attract new customers, little data is readily available to help with the more profitable practice of improving retention and growth from the current customer base. Companies like FreshLime and Gainsight are exploiting this opportunity, but they need excellent transaction and CRM data partnerships to make this happen. Repurposing current data in your CRM or within your transactional data with help from partners like these can deliver significant business value.

Overall, the growth in CRM-related data solutions is powering a great proportion of the data partnerships companies need today. There are so many use cases here that we recommend you openly approach vendors within your CRM ecosystem about partnership opportunities. They are likely to be connected to dozens of companies comparable to yours that would benefit from working with you by sharing data and insight. If a CRM application can access your data and the data from 500 other businesses, it may know which other types of businesses and services share the same customers you have but don't compete with you. From here, it can connect the two of you to discuss a channel sales partnership or joint marketing agreement. These are some of the values delivered by extrinsic datasets used to identify partnership opportunities, whether with or through the platforms that aggregate or report on your company.

Employee and People Data

Employee data, payroll, recruiting, and any other system focused upon your workforce is an underutilized data source with substantial value. The proof is in the rise of some massive SaaS (software-as-a-service) providers in this space alongside the entrenched titans. ADP, long one of the most important platforms in payroll and employee management software, has been one of the most important providers of employment data to data partners and the financial services industry. By aggregating payroll data across millions of businesses, ADP provides a deep view of the health of various companies, industries, and markets.

The depth of data you have on employees varies based on how much you depend on human employees in your enterprise. Regardless, one area that you will have more data in than actual employee count is résumés and job applicants; these have become a new data source. Glassdoor, LinkedIn, Indeed, and ZipRecruiter are all working to formalize and structure the information trapped in PDF documents and résumés to free up the information and attributes that apply to candidates hired by, and possibly rejected by, different businesses. Companies like Glassdoor aggregate the employee information, capabilities, schools, accomplishments, interests, and roles of millions of individuals across hundreds of thousands of businesses. You can, and should, tap into the wealth of extrinsic employee data that LinkedIn or Indeed have about your employees, your former employees, and those who applied to work for you. At the very least, it will provide you with new insights into the characteristics of employees that your company attracts, and why they stay or leave.

There are other, perhaps less straightforward reasons to catalog this data. Of course, for most businesses, the actual data around their own employees is confidential and sacred, but you should consider partnering or purchasing additional data from sources like those listed above to help inform your hiring and compensation strategy. There are plenty of ways to reach out to these companies to work with them as a customer or as a contributor to their database. As this area grows, look for more ways to integrate employee data with transactional data, CRM, and financial systems. In other words, if your employees that work on Tuesday and Thursday evenings are the reason those nights have higher sales and more satisfied customers, the data can prove this. What happens from here is that platforms that focus on attributes around employees can then recommend other potential hires that have similar attributes to ensure you improve your organization. This is a highly data-driven approach to hiring and management. It's time to elevate this approach over classic, inefficient, "gut-reaction" hiring practices.

Operations Data

Operations SaaS and software companies are too numerous to list. In fact, we view the operational solutions category to also include data management, cloud infrastructure, document storage, and even facilities management. Most operational data and software workflow platforms started as purpose-built platforms built in-house by industry participants for their own use, only later to be turned into software solutions; this has generated an explosion of such platforms. This creates fragmentation in functionality, tools, and, crucially for us, data models. Because businesses have highly customized operations, flexible tools that can expand their data models or workflow systems are very popular.[16]

The alternative to these professional tools, which is still very popular, is using Excel, Google Docs, or another shared document structure that teams update in steps along an operational workflow. This approach is unfortunate because it leads to data errors, input errors, validation errors, and overall loss of fidelity. By using unstructured tools to manage operational workflows, even if you've modified them superbly, you end up with a few employees who own them because they are "masters" at how to track and use them. This makes sharing data difficult without the involvement of these operational gurus. We recommend you avoid this approach and instead, if you need a flexible platform, adopt one like Airtable or Trello that enforces a structured approach to your operational data and project and workflow management.

From the extrinsic data point of view, most operational platforms can export your content easily and many are extending their integrations to include other common business datasets like CRM, financial, transactional, and HR systems. The real opportunity here is to improve your business process management and efficiency. You can use aggregated industry standards and benchmarking to help make suggestions based on similarly situated companies. There are a lot of caveats and nuances with this type of external data; someone must examine it closely before it begins to generate much in the way of insights. The uniqueness of operational data points around steps, projects, and quality make it hard to generalize about data partnerships with operational data.

Companies that build and manage operational solutions and platforms — like Slack, Google Drive, Dropbox, and Jira — have been aggregating and improving their tools for years by analyzing the data captured in their systems. These same companies are beginning to expand their ability to identify potential data partnership opportunities that will help them and their clients.

---

16   Information Services Group, "Explosion in App Economy Transforming ADM," MarketWatch, September 7, 2018, www.marketwatch.com/press-release /explosion-in-app-economy-transforming-adm-2018-09-07.

Legal and Compliance Data

Legal documents with contract tracking have exploded recently as more and more businesses have awakened to the value of making the structured data trapped inside their contracts more accessible. From an internal data perspective, it can be quite time consuming to migrate to a contract management platform, but we know this is worth it. This type of system typically incorporates some operational and CRM workflow, to ensure that the data gathered is structured and repeatable.

The ecosystem of available datasets around structured contract data also creates many opportunities for partnerships. For example, online contract platforms like LegalZoom provide content, DocuSign provides signature tracking and workflow, and Apptus dominates price-to-cash management. Each of these platforms has integrations with additional third-party data platforms. They have turned what was once the boring world of seek-and-find through old contracts into a living data repository complete with contract dates, terms, financials, products, services, service-levels, indemnity provisions, renewals, and thousands of other data-rich outputs.

The world of compliance has been increasing its tools and datasets as well because of regulatory oversight and industry standards that require reporting and approval workflow. The data platforms in this space tend to address regulated verticals like financial services and healthcare. These industries manage compliance using broad platforms with complete oversight and content management and approval workflows. In financial services, Broadridge stands apart as one of the most expansive platforms, while in healthcare, it seems as if there are new documentation, records, and compliance companies created every day. Kareo, in Irvine, California, is one such platform for documents, records, billing, and marketing for small practices. Kareo has some of the best data in the industry due to its quality assurance and data ingestion workflows, which make sure that every procedure and service provided by practices is properly analyzed and matched to the appropriate insurance carrier codes. Firms like Broadridge and Kareo thrive because of the immensely complex data ecosystem that surrounds highly regulated businesses.

If your business operates under high levels of regulation, certification, and compliance, start to analyze where you store this information and how readily available it is to you. Also, begin the process of extracting the structured data in your contracts, regardless of your industry, to load them into an Airtable or a similarly structured data tool. By beginning this process, you will start to see some of the relationships between your own legal data and the other common datasets in your business.

Business development contracts that cover sharing data between two or more platforms have many common elements. The terms and contract elements are being analyzed constantly by these platforms and will soon be able to make suggestions to your team by analyzing similar language and terms across millions of contracts. Look to partner with these massive holders of extrinsic contract and compliance data to better inform your own practices.

Government-Related Data

As we discussed in the previous chapter, every business creates data and provides it to some sort of government entity or tax authority. That said, the government itself, particularly in the United States, is also one of the best sources of data available. With thousands of datasets provided at Data.gov, the government can provide insight on consumer trends, housing, climate, demographics, voting, employment, and many other topics. If you really want to know if consumer complaints are affected by rainy days, you can download both the consumer complaint file and the daily precipitation file and figure that out pretty quickly.

While the government is an outstanding and free data provider, its data has limitations, as does its use. You must obey specific terms and conditions, but that should not diminish the value of this outstanding resource. Timeliness is the main limitation of government data. Most governments gather information annually, or at best monthly. This means that you are always delayed in your ability to make forecasts or insights.

Tap the resources at Data.gov as you journey further into the data partnerships strategy mindset. By sifting through this site, you will see opportunities to interconnect with their continually improving data.

Local governments are starting to scale up their data efforts, which creates more partnership opportunities. Smart towns and smart cities need data partnerships to produce better experiences for their residents.[17] Real-time transit data, community events, and even emergency services are benefiting from data partnerships with businesses. If your business has a lot of local knowledge or information, reach out now to your local markets to begin the discussion of partnering on data. Naturally, governmental platforms are very concerned with privacy regulations, and they most definitely will take the humanized approach to sharing data, but most towns and cities will see the benefit of managing a data-rich platform where relevant content and information is available to the electorate.

Product and Inventory Data

Product and inventory data has become one of the largest and most complex areas of data management. Product data has expanded to incorporate almost every aspect of a product, not just its price or description. This dataset expansion is due not just to a need to know more about products, but also to a massive increase in the actual number of products. There are over 22 different varieties of Jell-O in the three-ounce-size box. Orange, strawberry, pomegranate — you name it, they make it. (When Jell-O was initially brought to market in the early 1900s, it only came in four flavors.) Variety, size, choice, and marketing drive an increase in the diversity in product databases, and this trend is accelerating. Soon, personal data, health data, genetic makeup, and thousands of other datasets will enable mass product customization. Artificial intelligence (AI) is going to fuel the custom product revolution further. To learn more about this "unscaling" trend, read *Unscaled: How AI and a New Generation of Upstarts Are Creating the Economy of the Future* by Hemant Taneja.

Along with this ability to customize a product, whether from an adapted messaging perspective or from an actual, physical transformation, there comes an exponential increase in the number of products and the data that describes them.

---

17   David Raths, "6 Organizations Make a Big Impact on Smart Cities," FutureStructure, September 1, 2018, www.govtech.com/fs/news /6-Organizations-Making-a-Big-Impact-on-Smart-Cities.html.

Amazon is at the forefront of product data and is an excellent potential data partner for anyone creating, selling, or distributing products. Thankfully, there are open and transparent resources from Amazon regarding how it stores and displays its product catalogs. As we write this, Amazon lists over 400 million different products available for sale on its platform, and that number continues to climb.

From a platform perspective, any data created by your business around products is an asset that you can exploit. What you sell, how often it sells, who buys it, for what purpose, when, and at what price are all important metrics that you should store indefinitely in your transaction file. Resist the temptation of just entering the bare minimum of information into your point of sale system or web content management system when it comes to your products. Particularly if you are the inventor and manufacturer of the product, you should embrace the notion that information equals discovery and ultimately sales. The more information and details about your products you can provide, the more likely you will see success in marketing and selling your product.

Inventory, as a subset of product data, is the actual amount of product you have available and how often it turns over. This information is very popular with partners because there are many businesses, investor research platforms, and manufacturing consulting firms that want to understand a product's lifecycle. The best ways to access and share this information is through the transaction log file from your point of sale system, where inventory and sales can be exported over time for a particular product. Your company can then provide this information to your data partners who want to understand how fast every car, tire, toy, doormat, or any other product makes its way through your business to the ultimate end customer.

While the vast majority of data created in products and inventory records is intrinsic, the explosion in product data has spawned a whole ecosystem of supporting extrinsic datasets. For example, recommendation engines, long made popular in online checkout platforms, are taking all of the data you produce about your products and matching them with highly unique characteristics and interest data about users. These tools show "customers who bought this also bought that," and the technology of recommendations has come a very long way. Algorithms now tap into AI wherever possible to suggest products to customers throughout their research, discovery, selection, and checkout process. The fuel for these algorithms is masses of transaction, product, and inventory data normalized across different platforms. If you own a restaurant, for example, a great suggestion engine will need to know what menu items, what ingredients, what wines, what cocktails, and what quantities of your inventory are consumed and at what times. When analyzed over thousands of restaurants and geographies, this data can generate some specific and valuable insights, helping drive data-powered suggestions.

Extrinsic partnerships in inventory or product-specific content will continue to benefit as providers expand the possibilities of customization. Look for applications that identify the differences in product data to custom fit or select, or those that recommend your product to the right people. Knowing that positive recommendations are much more likely when the product fits the customer's goal will, in turn, drive more interest in the product. The future of retail and product design is customization to the millimeter and the constant feedback loop that you can help power through data collection and partnership. Take the tour of the algorithm behind the success at Stitch Fix to get a glimpse of what this means for retail apparel and accessories.[18]

Manufacturing Data

Data around manufacturing largely hinges upon the products and the supplies required to produce those products. Commodities, access, shipping, and delivery information drive studies in efficiency and value. Because of this, there are large numbers of manufacturing datasets on Data.gov. For most scenarios, if your business manufactures goods, the valuable data you will possess will be evident in some of the other platforms already discussed. For example, your vendors and suppliers are captured in your accounting and bookkeeping, while your operational systems will capture your manufacturing times and workflow. This type of information

---

18   "Algorithms Tour," MultiThreaded: Technology at Stitch Fix,
      https://algorithms-tour.stitchfix.com/.

extends up and down the supply chain, even unearthing the metals and core elements behind the products you create.

From an external data perspective, manufacturing is the lifeblood of companies, and subsequently, large swaths of the economy. For this reason, many investment firms and research houses seek to compile as much raw or first-party data about manufacturing costs and timelines as possible. They can then analyze this across industries or vendors to identify trends and help hedge for the future. If your company has a significant manufacturing operation, you should immediately consider what other industries that either supply or purchase from yours will benefit from having more complete data across your product line.

Shipping data is also a promising subset of the manufacturing process. Because the time in transit of both materials and finished goods directly affects inventories, availability, and ultimately revenue, many firms seek shipping- and transit-time data to help them forecast industry or corporate earnings. Platforms that allow you to track shipping and logistics throughout your manufacturing and delivery process can provide a valuable data asset.

In terms of extrinsic partnership opportunities, the process of creating a product touches a number of industries, geographies, companies, and governments. Take a look at a beautiful visual representation in which Kate Crawford and Vladan Joler map the metals, mining, and materials that go into an Amazon Echo device in a series called *Anatomy of an AI System*.[19] The map documents the massive collaborative effort across manufacturing, power, data, knowledge, and consumption, and it can help connect the dots to show just how expansive and connected partnerships have made the manufacturing process.

Social Media Data

The amount of external data that is produced around your business in the social sense is immense, and should concern you. From likes to retweets,

---

19   Kate Crawford and Vladan Joler, "Anatomy of an AI System," 2018, https://anatomyof.ai/.

the data created about your business in this medium can often dwarf the actual amount of data produced by your entire company and all of its operations. Consider a company with a social media footprint like Apple, which has millions of social posts, comments, and blog shares continuously created about it every single day. None of that data was produced by the company. The sheer volume of consumer and fan content overwhelms anything that enterprises themselves produce, and companies can take advantage of that content in many different ways.

Even for small businesses, the amount of social data created around their enterprise and available for review can be overwhelming. Social media, by its nature, is part of a relationship graph where every person is connected to others via location, interests, and thousands of other potential commonalities. For that reason, this dataset can be powerful for marketing and brand awareness. It's not just the Facebook page, Twitter account, and Snapchat tools that make these platforms valuable, but the opportunities to benefit from the human connective data in creative ways.

Take, for example, a product called HijackAds, powered by LocalStack, an independent technology firm in San Diego, California. HijackAds simply exploits readily available information about a business from social data. After a business enters its phone number into the platform, HijackAds goes to Facebook and uses the phone number to unlock access to the company's business page and followers. From there, it uses a proprietary algorithm to gather up all competing businesses around that business, using data on geographic proximity and category of business. Next, the platform finds all of the people on Facebook who either follow those competitors or have liked the competitor or interacted with the competitor's business on Facebook, along with their closest friends. HijackAds then creates an audience on Facebook that you can easily target ads to, thus reaching all of the people who are likely to have some involvement or interest in your competitors' businesses.

This is an excellent example of how social content created around your business can have enormous value, sometimes without your involvement. Interacting with consumers, fans, and any audience for your business is also getting easier. While it's helpful to gather data about customers, appended with demographics, income level, and propensity model scores, it's very hard to argue with the extra value that comes from ad targeting based on actual social interaction and proximity.

Even the growth in ephemeral messaging and sharing apps is an opportunity for an extrinsic data partnership. Whether it's on Instagram, Snap, Confide, or other platforms that allow for messages and photos to be viewed once and then disappear, the interaction data is valuable and can present an opportunity. Consider Snapchat, the app powered by Snap Inc., which pioneered the ephemeral messaging concept. Their platform knows the location of each customer and can share that data with advertisers because of its terms of use with consumers. This means that these typically young users can be targeted exactly where they are, in proximity to individual businesses. This approach uses a technology called geofencing, where a business can draw a polygonal shape on a digital map around their place of business, and when a user crosses the boundary to enter this shape, they become eligible to see ads or interact with the company through filters and advanced tools. Big brands are all over this capability, adding their logos to photos, or stickers, or just about any other clever tools employed by the Snapchat app. These interactions are fleeting in their lifespan but highly valuable because they connect location, time, and person. This connective layer of data enables consumers to engage with the brand's identity while still ensuring that their message content remains private.

Another use of this technology is to draw polygon shapes over your competitor's business locations or other places that are not your owned-and-operated store locations. This means that one home improvement chain can put a polygon shape over the parking lot of a competing home improvement business and target any customers entering that competing store's parking lot with an ad or coupon to induce them to come to their store instead. This practice, often referred to as "conquesting," even allows the user to easily share with their own followers that the store doing the advertising is offering something of value.

Social isn't just about friends, likes, tweets, or follows; it has become a global dataset that demands your attention as you look at your own data assets. Once your business has established its social presence, the comments and interactions with consumers and competitors will end up being a diverse and powerful dataset requiring your attention.

Location Data

Location data is all of the information about and around your business locations. Whether your company is a one-location local business or a 10,000-location mega-franchise, customers and visitors create an enormous amount of information about and around each location. While significant portions of this data are directly under your control, like hours of operation, menus, services, or even worker biographies, other datasets built *around* each location can be very useful and valuable.

Property values, rent costs, other tenants, and the changes in each of those are critical data points used by platforms like CoStar, Realtor.com, and Zillow. These companies compile real estate data and sell access to it to realtors and companies, helping them understand not only business location costs but also opportunities. Such location data informs decisions about where to open or not open stores, as well as other feasibility studies, and your business location data is included in these studies whether you want to participate or not.

Location data isn't limited, however, to just the financial aspects of rent and prices. For consumers, where a business is located, what it provides there, and when they can visit are all foundational data points upon which tons of other datasets are built. Most businesses have realized that any other dataset, whether social, transactional, financial, people, advertising, or whatever, can generate more insights if they attach it to or cross-reference it against the locations from which those datasets were gathered. What can businesses learn from examining which location sells the most sandwiches, or breakfast sandwiches, or perhaps which location has the most social followers, or even which locations' employees have the most influence on major social media sites? Take almost any dataset and plot it on a map for an eye-opening experience.[20] The extrinsic value created is usually a great living example of data partnerships.

Location is also all about map usage and map interfaces. For thousands of years, maps have been made to inform people of locations and

---

20   Peter Murray, "Forty Brilliant Open Data Projects Preparing Smart Cities for 2018," Carto, September 28, 2017, https://carto.com/blog /forty-brilliant-open-data-projects-preparing-smart-cities-2018/.

to aid navigation. They have now evolved into real-time, interactive platforms, sometimes even with augmented reality applications that can overlay information about a location or route directly upon our glasses or windshield. These enhancements are all driven by aggregating, combining, and refining location data and information. Because maps are also intuitive to human visualization, many of the applications discussed in this chapter incorporate map overlays in their design. Facebook, Google, Snapchat, GroundTruth, HijackAds, and many others have a simple map view designed to center around location data as a way to convey their functionality.

Companies that have leveraged maps and location data most dynamically include Apple, Google, Uber, Waze, Lyft, Foursquare, and HERE. Each has turned the map and the location data upon it into business advantages, from logistics to discovery, and they will continue that refinement. For your business, it is important to understand that time and place, as two concepts, will continue to drive most of the marketing tools and sales solutions of the future. After all, where a consumer is, and what time it is, are two of the most promising ways to determine how to interact with potential customers and target them appropriately while minimizing personal data use. Location data is at the center of this trend.

One company that embodies the opportunities in data partnership around location data and other valuable business content is Yext.[21] Now a global operation, Yext originally focused on helping businesses be found on maps across various navigation platforms and online directory services. This has evolved to now include deep knowledge about a business, and in turn provides feedback from hundreds of platforms and applications back to the business. Hospitals and healthcare platforms can know which office each of their doctors is located in and then share that data directly with customers through connected applications and even Amazon Alexa. This type of real-time knowledge and connectivity is based upon a massive network of data partnerships in which information that is commonly needed to create amazing customer experiences can be shared in real time.

---

21 Again, Christian worked at Yext for years and is probably biased, but he doesn't think so, which is why Jay wrote this footnote.

Review Data

Reviews are typically about products, places, or people. While there are also review platforms focused on brands, these still tend to actually reference the people, products, or places associated with a company. In other words, plenty of review sites may have a contributor say, "I love Apple," but very rarely is that the end of the story. Instead, the contributor lists the products or services provided by Apple that they are so enamored with.

We credit Yelp with driving the review revolution. There were reviews and comment threads before, but Yelp successfully codified the process and the solutions and they continue to innovate to lead the space. Yelp began with human curation to identify truly helpful and unique reviews content and then opened up their platform to more participants and businesses themselves to create an ongoing dialogue about experiences. Depending on their reviews, businesses have hailed this as outstanding or derided it as villainous. The reality is somewhere in between, and depends on which end of the comment stream you find yourself.

Beyond Yelp, however, there are other important platforms and businesses that operate in the reviews space. The ecosystem of products to monitor, respond to, and help generate reviews is continuing to explode. This is a challenge. Reviews are a sensitive topic for businesses because many are false, misleading, and downright ugly. Businesses have to deal with the reality of living in a world where every opinion can matter. Business owners and operators have to deal with reviews, warranted or not, and the platforms and innovations in this space to do so will continue to multiply. The benefits of engaging even the most irate reviewer have been proven (often providing the most popular of interactions[22]). Our favorite book covering the proper interaction and method for dealing with detractors is *Hug Your Haters* by Jay Baer.[23] Regardless of your willingness to engage with reviewers, extrinsic data created about your company and hosted or disseminated by review platforms will impact your business.

---

22 David Weinfeld, "5 Best Responses to 1-Star Reviews," Rail, December 26, 2016, www.therail.media/stories/2016/12/26/5-best-responses-to-1-star-reviews.

23 Jay Baer, *Hug Your Haters: How to Embrace Complaints and Keep Your Customers* (New York: Penguin, 2016). See also www.jaybaer.com/hug-your-haters/.

TripAdvisor, Bazaarvoice, Podium, and Trustpilot all operate in the review space, but in very different capacities. The important thing to understand is that reviews, in general, create substantial amounts of extrinsic data that can create business opportunities. The timing of reviews, who wrote them, on what subject, and every other data point attached to a review can bring insights that your business needs. A consistent, well-planned strategy to respond to reviews is absolutely necessary for any business.

Traffic Data

No matter what the business, it has traffic data. Traffic can be both online and offline; there are visitors to your business's digital presence as well as to its physical locations. The first step in tracking traffic is setting up and maintaining your online and offline presence. By online presence, we mean the websites, social sites, directories, maps, and other content platforms that will identify and direct users to your business. By offline presence, we mean the locations, service areas, conferences, signage, and other real-world manifestations of your business where people can interact with your products and services. From that point, there are many ways you can store this data for use and analysis later. As mentioned earlier, traffic data is inherently extrinsic because it is created by others as they interact with your content, products, locations, and employees. Data about traffic is created regardless of your company's involvement. Nevertheless, it is one of the most important datasets to align with because it demonstrates the interest and intent of consumers when it comes to interacting with your business.

In the offline world, there are several companies that monitor actual foot traffic with cameras and counting devices. Pittsburgh-based TrafSys is one such company that uses both hardware and software to count the actual number of people that walk into and out of a business location. Retail shops, casinos, transit authorities, and other businesses use this type of data to track their customers' interest level, activities, and relationship to advertising, product launches, and events at their business locations. This continues to be a promising approach and has begun to leverage AI and facial recognition software to add additional data elements. The personal data and privacy issues with this technology are substantial, but many businesses are extending this real-world identification capability. In addition to these camera-based approaches to offline traffic, phones and other connected devices offer increasingly detailed visitor data.

Cuebiq, Foursquare, and SafeGraph are all data companies that use the GPS signals from cell phones to track where people go and how long they stay in a particular place, also known as dwell time. By tracking a user's phone and dwell time metrics, businesses can move away from cameras and hardware for measuring traffic to working with third-party data suppliers for that information. The beauty of this solution is that other data about a visitor is also available, even as the tracking company maintains their anonymity. While these companies are continuing to build offerings using this method, there are lots of regulations and laws governing this type of data usage, for obvious reasons. That said, being able to measure foot traffic in real time as it relates to a physical location is a dataset most businesses should pursue.

A host of platforms track digital or online traffic. Google Analytics, Facebook, Yext, SimilarWeb, and every DMP platform can provide traffic statistics to help businesses understand how often consumers visit their digital properties. Digital properties extend far beyond just websites these days, with a business's brand and identity existing in apps, maps, and hundreds of other modalities. This is a key insight, particularly as the world moves to new platforms for discovery like voice assistants and artificially intelligent assistants. For brands or businesses, traffic means any and all unique interactions with a customer or with a user, regardless of platform.

Consider platforms like Amazon's Alexa, Microsoft's Cortana, Samsung's Bixby, Apple's Siri, IBM's Watson, and others that leverage voice and intelligence to inform customers and consumers. These tools take data about businesses and turn that information into answers, which in turn represent a whole new type of traffic. Traffic is no longer just about someone landing on a website. The idea has been extended far beyond that simple interaction to include the complete set of digital interactions with a brand. If a voice assistant recommends a local restaurant because of its close proximity, excellent reviews, and current seating availability, then that recommendation is as good as, or often times better than, any other traffic the restaurant's website might garner. That said, many of these platforms are in their infancy, and their reporting on traffic is similarly basic. It will be some time before traffic statistics from these solutions inform businesses, but that shouldn't prevent you from recognizing their growing importance and identifying which data strategies related to them might benefit your business.

Competitive Intelligence Data

Competitive intelligence is something every business wants, no matter its size or scale. From the local pizza parlor to the global pizza chain, all seek information on pricing, deals, capacity, social standing, financials, and growth. This competitive drive is enhanced now that many data companies can offer substantial amounts of insight into almost any competitor. External sources of competitive intelligence typically specialize in a particular dataset and offer plans so that businesses can purchase this information or incorporate it into their dashboards and analytics.

As we mentioned, Dun & Bradstreet has offered third-party competitive intelligence for over 100 years. They analyze credit and financials, and model countless other derivative metrics to tell you exactly where your company stands. This dataset has grown over the years to allow you to identify and target competitors' customers by overlaying D&B consumer data with D&B business data. Companies like Experian, LiveRamp, and Infogroup offer similar services.

Another platform commonly serving Wall Street investment firms is Capital IQ, a division of Standard & Poor's. This type of financial and information platform tracks the world in terms of companies, their products, and their competitive standing. Underlying all of this is an enormous, and ever-updating, repository of data. Thomson Reuters and FactSet similarly collect and share massive amounts of data. These companies have created global partnerships not only to amass their own direct data assets and collection methods, but also to provide a platform for third-party data companies to distribute their data to financial services end customers. These companies offer great examples of how to build data partnerships for sharing, purchasing, and selling competitive data intelligence.

Summarizing Externally Created Datasets

For every business, there are opportunities to either purchase service from or partner with third parties to increase the value of your data. By simply being in business, most companies create data that third-party companies then track and aggregate into metrics for benchmarking and forecasting. It doesn't matter if this is tracking the growth of sales in tater tots at restaurants or the growth in keyword searches related to increases in cholesterol levels, it is all gathered by external platforms for your eventual access.

Remember that it is helpful to look at each of the categories of data as a silo as you begin to identify the fields and values and variety you have. Try not to think of the customer, what they bought, where they live, who they are connected to, and how to reach them as a dataset about that customer. By looking at data from a personal perspective, you accidentally narrow down the analysis to what appears to be one use case, when it is actually four or five different data sources. Because each source of extrinsic data is an ecosystem related to your business, you should examine each of your internal systems, and then identify which external companies specialize in the data for the ecosystem for that source of data. Making connections across datasets is often a step you have to take later on, when you've properly wrapped your head around each extrinsic data source.

Now that we have taken stock of intrinsic and extrinsic datasets, it is time to value your data.

Part II: Value

5

Valuing Data Assets

Once you have completed the analysis and audit of your business's intrinsic and extrinsic data assets, you can begin to assess the value of this data. While there's no method to create an exact valuation of your data, we will outline several classes of data and what makes them valuable. You can use these guidelines as a framework to analyze and construct your data partnership strategy.

From a purely legal standpoint, the valuation component of the DataSmart Method is crucial, because it allows you to identify the value of data from two perspectives: from your company's viewpoint and from the perspective of the customer, supplier, or other entity to which the data pertains. It's no mystery that you want to know how valuable the data is to you. But it is also important to consider how important the data is to the person who created it. A Social Security number that you have collected may be of limited or no value to you, but it is of enormous significance, legally and psychologically, to the data subject who gave it to you. The disparity in importance there should be a red flag for you, and we'll describe in this chapter what to do when you encounter that kind of value divergence.

The other benefit of going through a valuation exercise is that it will force you to rethink your overall data strategy. As we'll show, companies valuing their data should move through a discovery process that uncovers the need to change the way they approach their data gathering and storage, and access to datasets created by or about their business.

Identifying and valuing assets is a continuous process. There is never a final value, just a value that applies at a point in time, a value that will shift as you refine your approach and increase the depth and breadth of your data. From the perspective of building data partnerships, every potential relationship is unique, and the data trash of one partner can certainly be the data treasure of another.

The Four Buckets

We recommend that you approach your valuation process with a clear set of potential outcomes. This enables you to set ranges of realistic values to help you prioritize your efforts. Analyzing hundreds of different datasets over the years, we have witnessed a seemingly infinite number of proposed pricing structures and valuations. Companies set values based upon the quality, depth, breadth, uniqueness, and a host of other metrics. They also set pricing based upon who is buying the data and what they are willing to pay. An identical dataset can be sold to two different companies for vastly different dollar figures. However, there are some common themes in valuation in partnership structures, and to keep your process moving forward, we recommend you use the four "buckets" approach. The four most common "buckets" of value are:

- $0 Bucket: Barter or Commoditized
- $10K Bucket: Valuable or Nascent
- $100K Bucket: Highly Valuable or Established
- $1M+ Bucket: Unique or Critical

The general principle in any data strategy for valuing assets is that every piece of data must be viewed in terms of its unique value to the partner or buyer. For example, knowing whether or not almonds are in a particular restaurant's steak sauce may have little to no value to you, but to someone with an acute tree nut allergy, that piece of data is of enormous, critical value. Those valuing information, data, or knowledge must view it from multiple angles and understand it as an asset whose value transforms over time as both the data and the environment surrounding that data changes.

The four valuation buckets we've laid out will help you plan by focusing your attention on what opportunities are worth the most. For example, many companies or individuals subjectively value much of their current data at the $0 level, considering it to be not much more than the exhaust fumes of their daily operations or customer interactions. In one sense, they aren't wrong — they own plenty of data that no one would take in exchange for money. But it would be a mistake to think that data exchanged for zero *dollars* is data with zero *value*. On the contrary, a large amount of data in the $0 bucket is exchanged through barter every day in a variety of ways. For instance, consider virtually every free app in which a consumer enters private data, photos, videos, or other content and thereby shares rights to that data with the app creator. The consumer gives the app producer real-time location data and advertising preferences, the app producer gives the consumer access to Instagram or Pinterest or Candy Crush. No cash has exchanged hands, and so the $0 valuation holds true. In this barter relationship, there was no financial value from the consumer's perspective to photos they are sharing with friends or the candies they crush. But to the app producer, at scale, millions of photos per day or millions of captive screens for mid-game advertisements generates the $1 billion Instagram price tag or the (even more astonishing) $5.9 billion price tag for King Digital Entertainment, the creators of Candy Crush. Each party in the data valuation will have different opinions as to the value of the data exchanged. The exact same data on an individual basis may be worth nothing, and the app is likely free to download in the App Store, but the valuation at scale of the company producing the app is in the billions.

As we work through each valuation bucket, take notes about your company's current and potential opportunities in each valuation range, using the methods we described. The goal of this approach is to find more value in each of the valuation buckets to make them more attractive to partners. Put another way, you should be using the methods we outline to identify ways to turn a $0 dataset based upon barter into a $10K dataset, or a $10K dataset into one that sells for more than $100K. Move up the value chain in a meaningful way, wherever possible.

$0 Bucket: Barter or Commoditized

Don't let the name of this valuation fool you; this data still has value. The zero-dollar value refers only to the type of financial relationship between your business and potential data suppliers and partners. Just because you won't be charging any money to access this data doesn't mean it isn't valuable. In this bucket, while we are talking about data that you may not be able to sell, gathering it and sharing it can yield significant benefits at little to no cost. This data is typically used in barter transactions or as fuel for partnerships.

Most applications gather data as people use them. Mobile apps supply location data and other data points about the user in addition to whatever app functionality the user is gaining access to. This type of data is at the center of some of the biggest data assets in history. Facebook's media, Uber's driving patterns, Airbnb's property locations, and Twitter's content impact are all examples of massive value created from, essentially, data freely provided by people's mere use of each application. It was only through the combination of these datasets — which, again, someone else decided were not worth charging for — and the creative interpretation of their meaning that Facebook, Uber, Airbnb, and Twitter were able to create their empires.

Start with any of your intrinsic datasets identified earlier and analyze whether there is content or information that would be helpful to an extrinsic data platform partner. From here you should move through each dataset you have to identify whether there is data that can be useful to these third parties or that might present an opportunity for a barter partnership. While some of the data you have identified in step one of the DataSmart Method is personal information, you may still be able to use some of it in an anonymous or aggregated fashion. If your platform or business creates a large amount of data or content, you are likely producing significant $0 bucket data suitable for exchange.

Connections between your intrinsic data and other platforms focused on similar extrinsic data will allow your company to quickly explore some of your first data partnership opportunities. The beauty of this type of value is that your business can gather this data relatively easily by just continuing to store the data produced in your normal course of business. You should adopt simple data retention strategies for this exact purpose. Then, by identifying platforms or partners that are willing to share a product or service in exchange for you sharing this data with them, you can begin the process of expanding your access to data assets. Consider many of the companies and platforms discussed in chapter 4 that have industry-level benchmarks or content sharing arrangements. They will definitely consider a partnership for the right type of data, uniquely gathered by your operation.

Another great thing about $0 or barter data is that it keeps negotiation time with your potential partner to a minimum. Because this data's only value is through barter, the time spent on commercial contract clauses will be minimal. They get your data, and you, likely, get some data back that will help you run your business more efficiently. Interestingly, this lack of commercial consideration mirrors the way many consumers think about the data they share with businesses, apps, and platforms. Think of how little you thought and pondered upon downloading Facebook's app, or Instagram's, or the Weather Channel's app before installing it onto your phone. There's a pretty good chance you saw the price of $0.00, sized up the potential value as greater than that, and clicked the "install" button all within a fraction of a second. Then you began to enter personal data, information, or real-time location data from your phone into each of these platforms, making their aggregated dataset more valuable.

There are a couple of issues to keep in mind with $0 data partnerships. First, the process of sharing or not in these scenarios tends to have very little urgency. Paying even a little for something does have the benefit of immediately causing the buyer to seek value and interact with the data or platform right away. Payment creates urgency in both directions. Whether buying data or selling data, each party has an incentive to demonstrate value quickly to ensure an ongoing relationship. The $0 relationships lack this sense of urgency, which can cause a painfully slow process in the growth and exchange of value. In the consumer world, many platforms and apps spend marketing dollars to convey their value. They are seeking to create a sense of urgency, even though no monetary value is exchanged.

The second challenge with $0 partnerships is your ability to reclaim or remove your data. In most cases, when you barter data for value, with no real contract or negotiation, it's hard to get it back. In other words, everything a consumer posts to Facebook and Instagram and Twitter becomes, once posted, essentially in control of these platforms to keep and utilize forever. Consumers are realizing they can challenge this from time to time, but their acceptance of terms in a $0 agreement places strict limitations on their ability to remove data. The same is likely true for a data partnership where the purpose is to barter one dataset for another. If every business could just remove the financial data that they had shared with data companies, then the very benchmarks and industry insights derived from those submissions of data would cease to be accurate or valuable. How much would Facebook be worth if every user deleted their account and all the history and content ever associated with it?

You have to consider a negotiation strategy around your $0 bucket that will ensure you have flexibility. You also have to recognize that the people who actually generate your $0 data may place a substantially higher value on the data than you do. For instance, although it costs you very little to bundle and sell data about your own operations, if that data includes information about your employees, their opinion of the value of the data from a privacy and confidentiality standpoint may be substantially higher than zero. In fact, the data may be protected under any one of more than a dozen statutes ranging from Health Insurance Portability and Accountability Act (HIPAA) to the Family and Medical Leave Act (FMLA). In that way, the regulatory and personal value of the data you have can diverge sharply from the valuation you've given to the data.

At this point, let's revisit the red flag we discussed earlier where the value perceived by one party for a dataset is substantially different than the value perceived by a second party. Try to view every dataset through the humanized lens to see that transactions, locations, personal information, and other data fields often represent an individual and their actions. To that person, the value of that data may have significant value. While it may be simple to say that a detailed customer list has high value to your company, it is likely that this list might have an even higher value to the individual customers (given that their personal information is there). New regulations like the GDPR in Europe and the California Consumer Privacy Act have a lot of restrictions on what data can be shared or processed by third-party partners without disclosure and ongoing reporting. When it comes to $0 data, and every valuation bucket, companies must weigh the value of what they are receiving against the potential risks associated with certain data types.

While these valuation divergences are red flags, they're not stop signs; on the contrary, you should leverage your data in every ethical way that makes sense for your business. But we want you, prospectively, to evaluate the risk if the data is somehow compromised or breached, and to incorporate the costs of proportional security measures for each dataset. This applies with even greater force when you're discussing data from European citizens, in which case you may well have to consider the valuation that both the data subject and the regulator would place on the information. Even if the data subject believes that their IP address is worthless and it's a $0 dataset for you, a Data Protection Authority may (and, in fact, will) consider IP addresses to be personal data subject to the full range of protections set forth in the GDPR.

You can see, perhaps, why we believe that the "value" step in the DataSmart Method needs to come early. If you don't take the time to ascertain whether and why data has value, you will either have to undertake a time-consuming retrofit process later or you'll run the risk of proceeding with a data partnership that distorts the true value of the data at issue. Of course, the most important aspect of valuation is the internal one: how you categorize and evaluate the worth of the data you plan to share. But by recognizing the other important stakeholders in the process, you can maximize the impact of the valuation exercise.

$10K Bucket: Valuable or Nascent

The vast majority of datasets that companies believe are valuable reside in this valuation bucket. Many companies sell datasets for around $10,000 per year, or in a similar range, as part of their business. The beauty of these datasets is that while most sales are only in that $10K range, they are an inexhaustible resource; companies can resell them an unlimited number of times to an unlimited number of different customers. The data in this valuation range is best described as valuable but not necessarily unique. It is also nascent in that the value of the data is often just beginning to be understood.

Over the past 20 years, we have met, analyzed, and partnered with hundreds of businesses with a dataset in this valuation bucket. Examples are most typically where a company has identified that the very nature of their core business produces data that may be of value to financial service firms or investment analysts because it has a unique or insightful quality. Essentially, this means that some hedge fund has told them that they will pay for the data to test if it has any value.

For example, consider call centers that try to sell products to small businesses around the country. No matter what they are selling — let's say office cleaning services — they typically employ a dozen to a hundred people in a call center that dials out to thousands of small businesses a day and records the outcomes of those sales efforts. They log important data like whether the phone number was accurate, if they got to a human or just an answering service, whether a decision-maker could be reached, and other items appropriate to their sales efforts. For office cleaning, they might ask: "How large is your office?" or "How many rooms?" or "How many square feet?" They might also rightly ask, "About how many full-time employees do you employ that work out of that office location?" These questions are obviously important to selling cleaning services, but the answers create another altogether valuable asset in the form of employment and commercial real estate data.

There are many firms that have sales operations like this one that will dial, connect, and quickly attempt to sell to anywhere from 1,000 to 30,000 businesses a day. This means, in a typical month with 20 calling days, that they can generate a collection of first-party data on 20,000 to 600,000 businesses. The math adds up quickly. One hundred sales people, contacting a business every 10 minutes, 5 hours a day, quickly becomes 600,000 businesses contacted and their data gathered in one month. There are roughly 30 million businesses in the United States. This type of data collection can quickly start to provide detailed employment or square footage data on a large portion of those businesses. Additionally, some services like this only target certain industries, which further focuses their data collection, making it even more timely and valuable.

These firms can sell this data to direct users of this type of information, like commercial real estate firms or employment benchmarking services. They may also sell a list of the subset of businesses that don't use answering services and have a decision-maker accessible. Think of the time savings for other sales companies that could skip making 30,000 phone calls, of which 20,000 don't reach a decision-maker. For some sales calls, this would be a drastic improvement in efficiency, and so long as the data is good, there are buyers for that information.

In this way, the natural course of business and sales calls can be made to serve a data need as well. Several outsourcing sales platforms do exactly this to identify better leads and qualifying data, then resell through third-party data-aggregator platforms. They offset some of the costs of their sales organizations by monetizing these data points. Most importantly, because every phone call has already reached an end state of "sold" or "unavailable" or "declined," these businesses haven't affected their ability to place their sales efforts first, knowing that everyone who buys this scrubbed list from them will be calling *after* they have made their attempts at sales.

Datasets in this valuation bucket are rarely the sole source of revenue for the businesses that produce them. When they are, these are more frequently lifestyle businesses than companies attempting to build scalable data platforms. While these solutions and datasets have some value, they are unlikely to be differentiated enough to break into the next valuation tier. One way in which these smaller amounts of data can achieve higher values is through a co-op approach in which several providers pool their similar sets of data. This happens in many different industries, and the concept is pretty simple. If a chain of delicatessens can track which beverages and brands of chips are selling most commonly and with the highest velocity at each of its 100 locations across the country, this is an interesting dataset on sales of those products. However, what happens if that same chain then combines this data with 100 other chains of restaurants, with a total of 10,000 retail restaurant outlets now recording sales of every bag of chips or beverage type? We are now talking about sales figures that provide valuable insight into trends and consumer preferences on an industry-wide scale. This co-op of data can then be sold to Wall Street investment houses that are studying Coca-Cola, Pepsi, and every other private or public manufacturer of beverages or chips. Data co-operatives like this are usually created by a company already selling a particular dataset, once they realize the potential of enhancing that dataset by approaching other businesses. These other businesses may not have built a data monetization strategy but are likely to have the same data stored somewhere in their normal business operations.

"Aha," your lawyer will say (and Jay just did), "but what happens when you run into a partner that wants an exclusive license?" This $10K valuation dataset has a unique value all its own: it is eminently re-sellable — or, more accurately, re-licensable, in that your goal is to sell the dataset but not ownership of the data flow that produced it. If you can sell one of these datasets to a customer in Poughkeepsie, you're fully capable of selling to another in Peoria. But occasionally, a potential partner will demand control over the dataset — not by owning the input but by restricting your right to resell to others. This is where the "exclusive license" comes into play, which effectively says, "I will buy your data, but no one else can."

Sometimes an exclusive deal is a deal worth making, especially if you can leverage it for a value greater than the $10K bucket. Perhaps you want access to a market that a partner is able to provide, or perhaps you are a small company that needs cash flow. There is nothing wrong with tactical decisions made to keep you afloat. But do bear in mind that your partner will want to maximize the amount of time that they hold the right to your data. Be aware of the potential long-term limitations that will come along with an exclusive arrangement.

$100K Bucket: Highly Valuable or Established

As we move up in our valuation, the next stage is reserved for datasets worth at least $100,000 per year, up to $1 million. Again, don't be too concerned about the actual dollar figure. Think about orders of magnitude. These $100K datasets tend to be well established, with a high value that exists because others need access to them to create or run their own business or applications. For example, in order for many sales organizations to run efficiently, large companies need a clean dataset of business information data to pull leads from or to compare their sales data with. This is the type of dataset that is used to cleanse or augment their own data stored in their CRM, but it can have immense value in increasing their operational efficiency.

For years, this type of CRM augmentation has been handled by companies like Experian, Infogroup, and Dun & Bradstreet. These companies could and would demand hundreds of thousands of dollars a year from a large sales organization that wanted to add fields to their CRM data. This is an incredible time saver as it allows for a seller or junior salesperson to just enter an email address or phone number into their sales CRM, which then instantly matches up the data with a massive database, filling in all the additional data points the seller needs. From an email or phone number, the sales staffer gets a full record of business names, officers, locations, employee counts, annual sales figures, industry categories, and other fields that help describe the lead or prospect. This data has long been a staple good of most sales organizations, and it can command a high price so long as the data quality is solid.

Included in the $100K valuation level are some datasets that might otherwise seem unrelated to anything of value but, with the right insight, prove to be an important component of various investment strategies. For example, hedge funds and investment advisors have long paid for "alternative research providers" that provide data outside of classic financial analysis.[24] The alternative research providers sell information or data with very specific (and sometimes slightly odd) parameters, like a semantic analysis of every word in every bill pending congressional review that might affect a given industry, or analysis of magazine headlines to identify whether a business has appeared or will appear.[25] These datasets assist analysts' valuations of stocks, companies, energy prices, or any number of other investments as an addition to the standard research. But where classic research would come to a financial recommendation or investment thesis ("Buy stock XYZ"), alternative research is more about providing nontraditional analyses to augment or complement existing strategies. Having even slightly more insight in investing can yield an edge in returns, so firms are open to meeting with and purchasing from providers with this type of data.

---

24   John Detrixhe, "Selling Data to Feed Hedge Fund Computers Is One of the Hottest Areas of Finance Right Now," Quartz, September 20, 2017, https://qz.com/1082389/quant-hedge-funds-are-gorging-on-alternative-data -in-pursuit-of-an-investing-edge/.

25   The premise is that if your business is appearing on the cover of a magazine, it's either because you're in trouble and need to resort to PR, or because you're the bad news du jour. Either way, unless your CEO was in a glowing *Forbes* profile, the theory went, magazine coverage is an ill omen.

A great example of alternative research used for investment purposes are companies who specialize in high-resolution satellite photography. These companies have sold images of every major big-box retailer's stores, their parking lots, and all the malls around these lots. They sell these images to investment firms that analyze the number of cars in the parking lot from one day to the next. This technique was actually a breakthrough in predicting sales, particularly around shopping holidays like Black Friday in the United States. If the number of cars in the parking lots were seeing real increases at, say, a Target location, while not nearly as many in the Walmart parking lot across the highway on the same day, that was a predictive indicator of sales and, ultimately, the health of that business. It isn't hard to see how valuable that kind of information would be to Target, or to Walmart.

To be in the $100K valuation bucket, datasets must transition to a business model that scales and provides value to a sufficiently large market. While many companies begin with datasets in the $0 or $10K bucket, by building organizations or structures around the ongoing collection and refinement of their data, they can develop the datasets into a far more substantial asset. Going back to the example of the satellite-imaging companies, while in the first few years these companies only provided the photos to investment firms, many realized quickly that if they refined their collection methodology and actually provided the car counts (and now even the count of people in the cars) they could demand a higher sales price. Similarly, you should think about how to refine your data for easier use and ingestion or how to make it more actionable.

Consider LiveRamp, a company that specializes in helping large business-to-consumer companies manage and connect their data to other platforms. LiveRamp was started to tackle the major challenge of coordinating advertising across different ad networks and channels. Along the way, LiveRamp began to refine the data it collected, and began offering what it calls "identity" resolution. This is the process of tracking an individual consumer across different platforms or devices and browsers. By focusing on this refinement of the data and enabling new capabilities around it, LiveRamp began to provide the ability for companies to match their CRM data with browser sessions and to deliver ads based on the massive database that LiveRamp had stored around users' identities. This ability to jump between different platforms while still connecting to the same individual dramatically improved how companies could take advantage of customer data, driving LiveRamp's revenue and valuation skyward. To take advantage of this refined approach, Acxiom eventually acquired LiveRamp for $310 million and will make it a staple of their future data business.

When considering your own data assets, think about the amount of data you possess, how quickly it grows, and how it is gathered, stored, and made accessible. In the $0 and $10K valuation range, you'll mostly find that the amount of data is modest, gathering it is not systematic, and it's not easy to provide or scale access to it. The proper approach is to test selling or sharing data streams in these lower valuation ranges before expending significant amounts of time and money to increase the scope and scale of the data operation. For many large business-to-business or business-to-consumer companies, the amount of data they have is sufficient to suggest a value proposition, but it may not be as easy to determine how they could refine this data or make it more actionable for resale or partnerships.

One last thing about the $100K valuation range: upon reaching this level, there is a ticking clock on your business. Most companies that get to this point are successful in striking their first few large-scale sales or partnerships to improve their dataset and to refine it further. But many of these companies then get purchased before they can get much farther. Because this valuation range is the last step before much greater scale and revenue, many of the very partnerships you might seek to create will, in fact, highlight your value to much larger businesses that seek exclusive access to your data assets. LiveRamp, MapMyFitness, Flatiron Health, Cask Data, TickerTags, Datorama, Ring, Data.com, Fitness AR, Twizoo, MapData, Pattern: each was an acquisition with substantial data assets that were on a breakout trajectory. If you don't want to sell your business or be acquired, you need to accept that there will be some strain in your partnership with bigger companies and in data sales negotiations with major players that see the value in your data. If you choose not to sell your company to them and are unsuccessful in striking a meaningful business relationship, your choices will likely spawn your next competitor; large and well-funded data businesses don't sit idly by while others create new data empires.

$1M+ Bucket: Unique or Critical

The last valuation range is less a range and more a statement of unique value at scale. Data businesses in this range have large complete datasets that generate actionable information and insights, allowing their customers to create or improve their own businesses. Think of global financial data, real-time weather, global map data, nationwide real estate availability, and autonomous vehicle routing data; all are transformational. Data providers who can successfully execute partnerships to sell this data will build lasting value.

Companies that reach this level typically find multiple industries or sectors that want their information. With licenses to the content in this valuation bucket costing over $1M annually, the key here is to have actionable, unique datasets that are large enough and of a quality level that ensures that customers purchasing the information can see clear improvement in their own products or services. Weather data, as we mentioned before, has reached this echelon where sales organizations, commodities producers and traders, marketing platforms, and Wall Street hedge funds all have found significant benefit in the dataset. It doesn't stop there, however; for a dataset like weather, there are countless new opportunities to explore, which is another reason why IBM acquired the data assets and digital properties of the Weather Company in 2005. Rising average temperatures and declining rainfall can inform significant long-term economic policy shifts; energy and manufacturing companies use the same data to estimate demand on their grids and supply lines. The use of great, universal datasets will always evolve farther, but truly massive data businesses have found that their data becomes foundational across various industries. This essentially makes competing in an industry without their data all but impossible.

Another common factor for companies that have graduated to this highest level of valuation range is their ability to spot great new data opportunities early. IBM, for example, once it had purchased the Weather Company's digital assets, began to rapidly refine and augment this data with other tools and content. IBM has become a phenomenal data platform, re-inventing itself around Watson, artificial intelligence, machine learning, and unique data assets like the forecasting models of the Weather Company. In fact, with the launch and expansion of Bluemix, IBM has pushed the concept of Platform as a Service (PaaS) to the forefront, enabling companies to not only bring their data to the platform, but to easily mash up their data with IBM proprietary data assets. Big Data, an admittedly overhyped term, is at the root of these PaaS developments. Face it: unless you are Google, Facebook, IBM, Microsoft, or a handful of other businesses with the staff and expertise to manage Big Data assets, you will need to rent or partner with these firms to gain any value from your Big Data. This is the model of the future, where data partnerships and services expand beyond a simple API connection transferring data between companies. The ability to manipulate data at scale is the direction most of the best data platforms are headed. Those that have reached this valuation range then continue to expand their empire by identifying great participants in the platform ecosystem they have built. They identify them, and then, wherever appropriate, they acquire their unique new datasets.

One consideration for businesses that find themselves in the fortunate position of holding such a valuable dataset is that they are going to be noticed — by competitors, certainly, but also by regulators. It is the businesses in possession of massive, valuable, leverageable datasets that often draw the closest scrutiny from government entities because of the potential for harm to consumers or misuse of the data. Consider, for instance, the GDPR, which singles out businesses whose "core activities...consist of processing operations which, by virtue of their nature, their scope and/ or their purposes, require regular and systematic monitoring of data subjects on a large scale." Those companies must appoint a data protection officer, who then has to liaise with EU authorities on data protection and must provide extremely detailed records to those authorities on what it is the company is doing with all that data. In the United States, the FTC pays very close attention to what large-scale data processors are doing, as do other regulators like the Consumer Financial Protection Bureau (CFPB), Federal Communications Commission (FCC), and SEC. With great success comes great scrutiny, so as you scale your business and secure a $1M+ dataset, understand that you will be in the spotlight.

Degrees of Value

Data asset valuation is also based upon degrees of coverage, depth, freshness, uniqueness, and accuracy. Each of these can significantly influence the value of your data; you can invest in improving them. For example, if your data is not comprehensive, or available across a large enough universe of coverage, you can work to increase your ingestion or gathering methods to improve on that dimension. The key here is that the different degrees of these qualities multiply the value of your data.

Begin with coverage: the ability to offer enough data in any given vertical or specialty is the first hurdle to overcome. There are two ways to view whether data represents comprehensive coverage. The first is to merely take a statistical viewpoint based on the industry. For example, you might remember those Crest toothpaste commercials years ago that loved to point out that four out of five dentists agreed that brushing with Crest toothpaste was helpful to oral hygiene. To most statisticians, this shows that 80 percent of dentists apparently stand behind Crest toothpaste, but that statistic never qualified whether or not the company had actually asked only five total dentists the question. Wrongly, people assume perhaps that the statistic is the common ratio of a much broader and more comprehensive study, but that wasn't made clear in those early television commercials. This gets to the heart of a comprehensive dataset. With about 200,000 dentists practicing in the United States, asking five would not offer a comprehensive analysis. In fact, at that point, not only do you have a serious extrapolation problem, but also potentially terrible teeth.

Having a comprehensive dataset really depends upon the purpose of your use case. If your dataset creates actionable information, then it is probably comprehensive enough. But if your dataset is really about providing a base layer of information, you will need far larger statistical coverage. This differs market to market, but 25 percent coverage starts to get interesting in most cases. If you are providing business location information on the United States, you need to cover about 5 million to 6 million business locations to be close to the 25 percent mark. If, on the other hand, you are only providing data on coin Laundromats in the United States, of which there are roughly 30,000, then data on 7,500 will be valuable.

Depth is the second factor of degree. Depth of data refers to the amount of quality information contained within each record. While coverage is the number of records on a given population, depth is the number of usable data fields tied to each record. For example, consider two different data files, each with 100,000 records that represent consumers in the United States. In the first data file, each record contains the name, address, and phone number of the consumer. The second data file contains the name, address, phone number, mortgage amount, own-versus-rent status, purchase history, propensity-model scores, credit ratings, education level, and about a thousand other potential data points that marketers use in ad targeting campaigns. The first file has the same coverage as the second, but the second has a significantly higher degree of depth.

Keep in mind that while depth can always be improved, it doesn't pay to improve it at the expense of fill rates and quality. Fill rates are defined as the number of values in each field for each record within a file. Adding more potential fields to create the illusion of depth is a common trick that data companies use to improve their datasets. These firms will say they have 100,000 records with 100 fields of depth, but what you will find upon deeper analysis is that their fill rates for each of those additional fields is very low. If you can't fill the fields, you should really consider whether you should market them as available at all.

Go on to assess the next degree, the freshness of your data. Just as in the produce section of a grocery store, there is significant value in data that is fresh, updated regularly, and not rotten. Naturally, you may not be able to control the freshness of your data, depending upon the industry, particularly around actions taken by others like the timing of purchases. Weather, traffic, and new home buyers, on the other hand, change and update every day. In some datasets, freshness is impossible to improve, and in others, it happens whether you want it to or not. The key is to identify the absolute best level of freshness possible given your dataset and to strive for that. In commercial real estate databases, this means you can only update square footage pricing as and when new leases are signed, but the market will reward how fast you can update that data as it changes.

We analyze freshness based upon the date and time stored next to each record that tracks the last time the record was updated. However, in modern data models, it is actually important to have an updated date and time next to every field of data within a record. It is no longer sufficient to say you updated a consumer profile last week. Your data model needs to be able to point out which field was updated last week, because data strategists have learned that updated records are easily manipulated without any true additional value or change in the valuable fields. Also, most models are now multivariate, meaning they can consider several variables at once and weight them based on their freshness. In this way, a consumer record with an updated phone number last week can be recognized as not as high a priority as a consumer record with an updated physical home address yesterday.

Differentiation is more of a marketing term than a definable attribute of a dataset. However, it is a critical degree multiplier for data. I've worked with several firms over the years that could demonstrate the unique nature of their data. If that unique data was actionable, it increased the market value of the data. One company, Target Data out of Chicago, was able to analyze every real estate listing and sale in the United States to extract specific attributes that allowed the company to predict when a private home or residence would sell in any given market. This derived dataset is powerfully unique because of its scale and depth but also because it included thousands of unique factors, like its formula for "granite counters" in a real estate listing in a particular zip code. That said, every dataset marketed as unique will fast find competitors seeking to mimic it. Your data collection methods, depth, coverage, and fill rates are all ways to keep your unique value proposition strong.

Accuracy is the last degree we analyze, but it is the measure by which many a data firm has thrived or perished. Data sources should have quality measures included with their data, especially now that customers or data partners can check data at scale so easily. Companies can easily lose sight of how important accuracy is. When building out your data collection, storage, and delivery methods, you need to build quality checks and controls into the process itself. For example, if you take data from customers or app users, do you enforce field validation in your forms? This is the process of ensuring that a zip code is entered as an actual zip code and a consumer can't enter "puppy" into that field. Even if you enforce this sort of validation, it is highly unlikely that you enforce the same level of field validation for your own employees' access to the data. This has caused many an issue for companies, sometimes going way beyond a data quality problem.[26] We discuss role-based account controls, which ensure data quality isn't accidentally or intentionally changed by internal personnel, in chapter 12. Most companies who are serious about their data strategy employ a chief data officer to improve data quality across every step of the collection, processing, and internal use. Companies must employ data checks, validation, and controls at all points in the creation of a dataset. To allow employees to bulk upload, bulk change, or bulk update data without the same controls threatens accuracy. The belief that one's employees don't make mistakes is a hallmark of a poor data strategy and an invitation to error.

The degree of value attributed to coverage, depth, freshness, differentiation, and accuracy depends on the audience. Marketers who buy data by the pound for mass direct mailings to consumers don't demand the same degree of accuracy or depth as Wall Street analysts accessing earnings estimate files for public companies. Part of your data strategy is to value your data and identify the value that the market puts on each of these factors. It is impossible to focus on all of these at once, so choose where you receive the most leverage and maximize your efforts there. Create a process and best practices that protect the data from manipulation or degradation at every step of your dataset creation.

Lastly, document your process and methods. By doing so, you can highlight your efforts as you market your dataset for sales and for partnership valuation. Data is like any other product, good, or service in that purchasers and partners want to have trust in the data, that it is fit for purpose, and that it can maintain the quality needed in an ongoing, protected process. Your next step is to present the data in a simple and elegant way.

---

26   Ashley Feinberg, "Comcast Changed Customer's Name to 'Asshole Brown' But Is Totally Sorry," Gizmodo, January 28, 2015, https://gizmodo.com /comcast-changed-customers-name-to-asshole-brown-but-i-1682409072.

Valuation Is Subjective

Now that you have a framework to approach your data assets, begin to take each of the datasets in your business and document them in a spreadsheet. Choose a valuation bucket — $0, $10K, $100K, or $1M+ — for each dataset based upon your first instinct. From there, add columns for each degree factor and assign a multiplier for each one, ranging from .5x to 2x, to start to arrive at a prioritization value in your last column.

This exercise isn't meant to tell you your data is worth exactly a certain amount of money. This is all about getting a directional view of where you need to focus your attention. No company does all of its data right all the time. Companies focus and specialize around their strengths. Focus on where you can improve either by increasing record count, fields filled, depth, quality, or any other factor to get the maximum leverage on valuation.

Once this internal exercise is completed, you need to reach out to a few industry experts or participants to begin a basic review of your findings and assumptions. We have had the unfortunate experience of having to explain to several hopeful data companies that their data is neither unique nor of a quality that would fetch anywhere close to the company's initial valuation assumptions. That said, we guided most of them to focus on other areas like depth and tangential datasets that they could easily gather that were, in fact, unique and valuable. In every case, this process is much easier and more effective if you do it after a complete audit of intrinsic and extrinsic data assets and then a preliminary assignment of value.

6

Presenting Data

To create the maximum value, urgency, and leverage in a data partnership, you must present the data available for sale or partnership in a clear and comprehensive way. Partnerships are based upon the concept that you are offering value for value, whether paid or traded. Friendship needs no reasons, but partnerships require some understanding of the exchange of value.

The most common way to reveal the value of data is to share three different files or documents, each with a slightly different view of your data assets. The first file, called the data brief, is a presentation or document describing your data assets and highlighting their best qualities and potential uses, or case studies of actual use. Your best strategy is to present this in person or, if that's not possible, in a phone conversation or virtual meeting. The second file is a comprehensive document called a data catalog that outlines all of the facts about your data assets. The last file is a sample data file to assist would-be partners to test your data. The brief, catalog, and sample files need to represent accurately and clearly the value of your data.

Companies that fail to present data assets effectively will also fail to attract partnerships and receive fair compensation for their data. The value of your data is not obvious. Unfortunately, those closest to the data, meaning you and your team, are also those most likely to become frustrated when potential partners' misunderstand the value of your data. To prevent that frustration, invest the time to create the brief, the catalog, and the sample file.

About the Three Files That Will Prove the Value of Your Data

The brief — the initial presentation file to highlight your data assets — need not be very long. To get potential customers or data partners to value the data appropriately, you should present it in simple terms, with appealing visuals that highlight the data assets clearly. If data can ever be considered sexy, this presentation should strive for that quality.

The brief needs to start with a simple definition of your dataset that describes it clearly; for example:

- The full semantic breakdown of the United States Patent library.
- The only user-generated, real-time gas price tracking platform.
- The deepest collection of consumer profiles for luxury item targeting.
- The highest-resolution hourly drone footage of US retail store locations.

Each of these sentences describes real datasets in their most appealing value terms. Focusing on the most important attributes, like "user-generated," "real-time," or "highest-resolution," highlights how the datasets are both unique and valuable.

From here, your presentation should draw out each major section of your data catalog, which is the second file you must create. Use striking graphics or "hero" numbers that clearly demonstrate the highlights in your data, such as the total number of records, how often the data is updated, quality metrics, and geographic or sector breakdowns. Each dataset has its own unique highlights.

In the second file, the data catalog, key sections include the initial data definition, the method of data collection, the refinement process, the commitment of quality, and the coverage, fill rates, and refresh rates per major data field. Your partner will appreciate it if you include a field definitions library at the end of the document, showing each field available, its data format (number, Boolean, date, currency, or text string, for example), its fill quantity (the percentage of records in which the field is filled), and a brief definition of what it conveys.

Your business and data teams should draft the initial brief as well as the data catalog, and your marketing department or agency should design them. This investment in clearly articulating what data assets you have will drastically shorten the partnership or sales cycle, immediately showcasing your data assets at a higher level than most. Many companies shortchange this effort and, as a result, never receive full value for their data. When you jump right to "let us send you a sample file," you miss the opportunity to build up your data value and control the dialogue.

You should create the final file, the sample, dynamically based upon the circumstance. While it's not usually necessary to customize the brief or the catalog, a custom sample data file will give each potential partnership its best chance at success. For example, for the drone footage company mentioned in chapter 5, if the company's executives are meeting with a major electronics retailer, they may want to exclusively show footage or population density visuals for similar electronics retailers. If the sample dataset has restaurants and Laundromats in it, this will reveal shortcomings to the potential buyer or partner. Their presence may show that the depth or coverage of the data file is inadequate, or maybe signal that the data owners are unable to deliver a custom dataset quickly and in a usable format. Most companies that are considering a data partnership or the purchase of data assets will have little patience with file delivery or formatting issues. This means that, prior to your first meeting, you should be prepared with a file that is likely to be appropriate to your audience, but also have a plan to quickly generate a different file if the meeting indicates a different need.

Relationship Mapping Values

The process of mapping relationships between your data values and those of the potential partner can cause countless misunderstandings and unnecessary delays. This is typically because each party has unique ways of looking at a business or person or product in their data; they need a Rosetta Stone of sorts to understand your dataset in their own context. This is central to the entire data partnership strategy for a business because there always needs to be a way to crosswalk from one dataset to another.

Here's how to highlight the most important components of your data catalog to streamline this process in each partnership discussion clearly.

Data, in any form, reduces the world to discrete values or ranges so we can efficiently understand and analyze the world around us. In other words, data is a description of, or the story of, our world. As such, every dataset can be related to any other dataset by identifying its key value when it comes to the classic questions of who, what, when, where, or why. Just as in your first journalism or writing class, these five factors are common ways to describe the world around us and to connect all of the elements of a story together.

By asking the following questions, both of your own data assets, and then of your potential data partner, you can quickly come to a common language to compare and analyze your data.

- Who is your data about?
- What is your data about?
- When did your data occur or change?
- Where (what location) is your data about?
- Why was your data created?

Is your data about people, products, or places? If so, each of those can be related to other databases with those as central themes. Consumer profiles, business locations, product codes, and medical reimbursement codes are all examples of common data anchors by which different datasets can be matched and compared. This means that who, what, and where are the most straightforward questions to answer, and you or your potential data partner can usually match corresponding data elements so that they can compare your data to theirs and thereby analyze your data's value. Every data record needs to correspond to the same person, product, or place across datasets. (The complexity of matching and match rates is beyond the scope of this book; if you need more detail, consult your database experts.)

Time is another fantastic way to connect data assets. When two datasets don't describe the same person, product, or place, time of occurrence or change is the next most likely area of correspondence. This is how drone footage and satellite imagery are tied to product sales at a retail store, for example. The photos of the cars or pedestrians in the parking lot of a retail store can be compared to transactional data from the store, because both have time stamps. While photos of parking lot density can't directly be tied to a product SKU, they can be compared to the times a particular product or series of products is purchased. Time is a universal connector that powerfully connects seemingly disparate datasets.

The last and most complicated data relationship to map, in both data and in writing, is around the question of why. The best way to think about how this matches up your data with other datasets is to try to match up sentiment or indications of interest around an event, product, or service. For example, many firms like Yelp semantically extract the sentiment of reviews left by patrons at restaurants and hotels, sentiments that can help answer that "why." When a reviewer of a restaurant leaves a comment like, "You have to try the 1-pound meatball appetizer, it's amazing," Yelp can relate the object of the meatball to a positive consumer experience and the subsequent recommendation of that business to others. This is one of the hardest elements to resolve in data collection, but the increasingly easy access to user interest and sentiment through mobile phone apps has created a whole new world of "why" relationship mapping.

Data Through Time

When presenting data assets, reviewing changes over time is a powerful magnifier of value. Charts of daily, weekly, monthly, quarterly, or annual shifts put your data assets into a common perspective. Most data briefs and data catalogs show the growth of their data assets — records, fields, or fill rates — as time-based series. Because most data collection efforts are cumulative, they grow over time, which attractively demonstrates their value. Make this accumulated value clear by identifying how many data-sets you have, and when each was created. Charting growth over time can also be a great way to highlight your lead over competing data suppliers, and how long it would take for a competitor to recreate your data at the same scale. For this reason, your brief and data catalog should convey how your scale or head start creates dominance in your space.

Another important temporal view of your data will reveal changes or updates to your data and when they occur. To highlight just how dynamic your data assets are, create scatter plot diagrams that show fields, how often they update, and how often they change. This insight can visually help a potential partner to understand not just the need for your data, but also the need for refreshing their feed of data from you on a timely basis. Some data suppliers will want to convey this early on in a discussion, because their potential data partners may have trouble ingesting data frequently. Partners' legacy corporate data structures and slow compilation practices can create barriers where, even if your data is amazingly useful, a data partner may not be able to ingest it fast enough to use it properly. This is why a chart of the frequency of updates is very helpful early, enabling you to demonstrate your capabilities to a potential data partner. Frequency charts also help your partner understand just how large of a data inflow they may be purchasing. It is a sad discussion when a data partnership is abandoned after weeks of discovery only because the receiving party realizes they can't ingest the fire hose of content you might be able to provide.

In the previous chapter we mentioned the need for storing the date and time for each update in your data. This is where that effort really shines in the data partnership strategy. Work with your technology teams to ensure that creation, updates, changes, confirmations, and deletions of every data field are tracked and time-stamped. This will highlight your freshness in your data value presentation.

Sharing and Mutual Non-Disclosure Agreements

Ultimately, the goal of preparing the three files of the data brief, catalog, and sample is to convey the value and purpose of a data partnership to your potential partner. Once you have these three files ready to go, here is the process that will make discovery and negotiation most effective.

First, present the data value in person if possible. Depending upon what industry or data specialty you reside in, this initial meeting may happen quickly, or it may take a while to set up. To speed the process, you may want to convey some of your initial value proposition early and, depending on the value of the data partnership to your strategy, you may even convey that you are willing to barter data for similarly valued data in return. This can take a lot of the "salesmanship" out of the discussion early, if, in fact, you are seeking to start with a partnership and not a sale. One strategy is to share portions of the data brief presentation in your first few emails along with an explanation of why you see a potential partnership creating additional value for both firms.

At the in-person meeting or video conference, your firm should walk through the entire data brief, promising to share the presentation after the call. This ensures you keep their attention on the discussion, because the goal is to learn as much as possible about their data business and needs. You should ask discovery questions related to each slide in your presentation to uncover the same information about their business that you are willing to share about your own. What is their current data about? How much data do they currently have? What is the refresh rate of their data? How do their fill rates look? Each answer you provide about your data should be followed by a discovery question to understand what they may have in terms of datasets.

While many meetings in Silicon Valley or San Francisco don't happen now without first completing a mutual non-disclosure agreement, or MNDA, you may be able to have the initial discovery meeting without one. You should conduct a thorough legal review with your counsel to determine what level of information you are willing to share before or after an MNDA is executed. That said, the MNDA is an excellent follow-up for any initial meeting between two potential data partners, because the MNDA is used as a stepping stone to the second and third files: the data catalog and the sample data file.

Who drafts the MNDA? Most large or public companies have a standard MNDA to maintain consistency across the organization. Regardless, if you are provided an MNDA by an interested potential partner, have your attorney review it and provide reasonable feedback. At this point, you may also get your first glimpse into what dealing with this company will be like should you continue the data partnership discussion. A company's MNDA can be completely mutual, or it can be mostly one-sided in their favor. In reviewing the document with your counsel, take note of what stance this counterparty typically starts with, as it is likely you will experience that approach as you continue negotiations.

When you are drafting your own MNDA, there are a few key points to consider. First, you should recognize that not everyone who wants to view your presentation is making a good faith effort to get to know your business. The risk is obvious: unsavvy company meets unsavory one and the crown jewels are stolen. This isn't likely, of course, and it may not ever happen, but you can't ignore the risk of a potential partner using your presentation to pilfer valuable data. The question to ask when you are being stonewalled about an MNDA is, "Why are they not willing to agree to mutually protect our interests?" If there isn't a meaningful or satisfactory answer to that question, then you are unlikely to go forward with a productive partnership.

Second, when structuring your presentation, remember that not all of your data has the same value. There are times when it may make sense to reveal some information without restriction (as an opening salvo) rather than to require everything under the sun to fall within the MNDA. You have to determine the value of the data relative to the benefits it provides and its status as a component of your presentation. If you think that giving a little information away will garner goodwill and help close a deal, it may make sense to exclude it from the scope of your MNDA; it's really a decision you have to make dependent upon the circumstances. There is no one-size-fits-all here. We have witnessed massive global organizations that have a completely healthy and fair-minded approach to disclosure agreements, while tiny shops that are terrified of sharing any data will sometimes request complete and total confidentiality around all aspects of their data.

To sum up, you need a thoughtful, step-by-step approach to what you share in terms of data. Some datasets refresh or change so quickly that a sample data file might be worthless in a matter of days (think of weather forecasts). Other datasets contain so much value that sharing them presents a conundrum about whether their value can be protected easily. These situations require thorough review with your attorney.

Part III: Structure

7

Legal Considerations

NOW THAT WE HAVE identified the general strategy for identification and valuation, it is worth examining the legal component of your approach to data and data partnerships. This means putting aside an entirely enterprise-minded way of thinking, and viewing the project through a legal prism. Lawyers and litigators approach problems from a unique perspective, likely as a result of their training. The reality of law school is not that you learn the law but instead how to "think like a lawyer."

To understand what that means, remember that lawyers spend every day engaged in lawsuits, suing or planning so as to not be sued, about everything from unpaid interest on a mezzanine loan to slipping on a banana peel. This certainly reinforces some of the paranoid-seeming beliefs from law school about danger lurking everywhere, but it also generates insight into what can, and often does, go wrong. As a lawyer becomes more experienced, they will begin to be able to come at problems from a different perspective, the "here's what I wouldn't do" point of view.

That may sound negative and unhelpful at first, but if you think about it for a moment, it makes sense. People hear all the time about why someone's pet project is a brilliant idea that will revolutionize the way we do business; it's a lot rarer to hear, "I like your idea, but here are some thoughts about how you can be smarter, safer, sounder."

In the end, your lawyer should be both advocate and counselor, someone who will argue on your behalf, but who also will help you understand different, and sometimes better or safer ways to accomplish your goals.

Our goal, when it comes to reminding you of the legal issues you face, is not to be, or to supplant advice from, your actual lawyer. Far from it — we are strong believers in the value of having a lawyer on your team. Instead, our aim is to offer some perspective about data partnerships coming from a legal point of view. By providing a basic understanding of legal fundamentals, we will give you a starting point from which you can build out a strategy that will last. If you create a relationship that is structured to allow for growth, change, or turmoil, you'll find that the elasticity you put into your contracts at the early stages will serve your company well down the line.

While this chapter provides the legal basics — the things you may or may not know — you should talk to your lawyer prior to starting any new venture. We'll start by looking at how the law treats business entities and enforces contracts. Then we will discuss the kind of legal protection your data has, from patented products to trade secrets. Finally, we'll examine what kind of issues newly formed partnerships have — particularly when it comes to arm's-length transactions. By the end, you won't have everything you need to strike out on your own and hang a shingle, but you'll be better informed than most, and you'll at least know where to begin.

Who Decides?

Before you consider the nature of your relationship with another business, understand what kind of business you are. Corporation, LP, LLP, LLLP, LLC, Partnership: each has its own benefits and drawbacks. For our purposes, the real question is how your business structure affects the way that you can enter into a relationship with a third party. For the most part, law in the United States is organized to maximize commerce and minimize hassle in contracts. Virtually any kind of company can, based on its own needs, enter into an agreement with any other kind of company, barring some special limitations (like subsidiaries or non-compete agreements). There are very few barriers to the idea of forming a data partnership. The practical side of making those agreements is where the issues arise.

Thus, for any given corporate structure, you have to understand who is allowed to make the decisions in your company, and how. A sole proprietor can do whatever they want; a partner may need to consult the partnership agreement; and a member in a manager-managed LLC is typically only the recipient of income/profits (the manager makes the decisions). Organizational documents (like articles of incorporation) often provide the necessary detail as to what kind of decisions the company can make and how. Read them before entering into partnerships.

Think of it this way: organizational documents are like a constitution for your company, and the law pretty much always requires that the constitution be enforced. So if you're the member in a manager-managed LLC and you try to make a contract with a data partner, your contract is likely to be worthless if the designated manager of the company doesn't agree. And if you're a general partner and you sign a contract with a black hat who steals all your data and your money, both your partner's personal assets and yours will be on the line, because there is no limited liability in a general partnership.

Using Data Derived from the Contracts You Already Have

Once you are comfortable that you have the authority to pursue a partnership and you've begun the data inventory process described in chapters 3 and 4, you're in a great position to start analyzing the relationships you already have. Most companies don't realize that they have a great deal of information flowing in from existing partners, even if those partnerships are not expressly data sharing partnerships. Consider, for instance, your distributors, affiliates, and similar partners — these relationships generate intrinsic and extrinsic data, of course, but they also depend on business relationships and contracts to facilitate those data flows. Understanding the contracts governing those relationships is essential to a complete data inventory.

It would be simple to just take whatever information you get from your third-party relationships and use it; after all, if the data is coming in, it must be yours to use, right? Not necessarily. All good contracts are specific about what rights and privileges the parties have, even if they aren't written in plain language. If you're dealing with a licensing agreement where you are only "renting" the goods or information you receive from a third party, then your rights are restricted. But even in non-licensing agreements (such as a standard supply contract), there can be language that curtails your rights. For example, most commercial contracts contain what are called "merger" or "integration" clauses, which say something like: "this contract is the entire agreement between the parties, superseding all previous agreements, and no modifications to this contract shall be of any effect unless in writing signed by both parties." The purpose of these clauses is effectively to prevent one party from later saying in court, "Yes, well, the contract says we get X, but we both agreed over a handshake that my company gets X, Y, and Z." (Free legal advice: people are liars.) A merger clause also serves, sometimes, to limit what the parties are entitled to under an agreement. If valuable data from your business relationship can be considered an asset or an interest otherwise covered by the terms of the contract, then you can't use it without the consent of your contractual partner.

There are endless permutations of this exercise. What about the data *about* the data produced by your business relationship? Is that yours to use, or does it contain proprietary information related to your partner in the contract? Is there confidential business information involved, such as in a licensing agreement? Sharing that data with a third party might not only be a breach of contract, it could also be a component of a copyright or patent infringement lawsuit. This principle extends to every piece of information that comes from your third-party relationships. If you don't truly know who owns the data or who can use the information, you're inviting risk. When it comes to data generated from relationships with other companies, be aware of the red flags that may come from licensing agreements.

Once you've identified the agreements and their important provisions, your next task is to identify your rights and obligations under each contract. This, of course, is something you will need to do with your lawyer, as every contract is different and there isn't any catch-all method to explain contracts. The key is the repetitive task of reading and rereading the contract until you and your lawyer are satisfied that you understand it well enough to make an informed choice. Don't be surprised if, each time you read the contract, you discover a subtlety (or, often, a typo) that escapes you on the previous passes.

And that's where the potential for litigation arises. The language of virtually all contracts is open to interpretation or challenge. I'll give you an example. The words "I promise to sell Jane Doe fifteen widgets for six hundred dollars" are an agreement, seemingly without any ambiguity. But did you say them out loud or write them in a document? If you don't have a signed document in writing, the law says that contract is likely unenforceable, because agreements for the sale of goods for more than $500 must be written. Also, were those US dollars? Do the widgets ever change or have different versions? And what about timing — the agreement doesn't specify, but what if Jane needs them immediately? Now you're headed back to court to figure out if the timeframe for selling the widgets was a "material term" of the contract.

My point is that conducting a data inventory or using data that comes from your existing business relationships may not be as simple as pulling together a spreadsheet. Until you have a firm grasp on what the agreements say and how they limit or define your right to use data, you must be extremely careful in how you proceed. This is particularly true if you did a decent job drafting the contract in the first place, with the result that it is advantageous for your company. The use of data derived from the other party, outside of the accepted contract, may be an excellent excuse for them to find a way out of the contract.

That being said, let's examine a systematic approach to reviewing your contracts (with the help of your lawyer, of course) to determine next steps for making use of intrinsic data.

Determine Who Is Involved

It's crucial to understand who your partner in the contract is. Sometimes, when you have a relationship with a third-party provider, that provider is a subsidiary of another entity, or may even be a single-purpose entity (SPE) that has no real substantive existence other than on paper. By focusing first on who is a party to the contract, you'll have a better idea of who the key decision-makers are (or at least be able to find out).

Identify Your Value Propositions

Every contract has terms that represent the most important aspects of the agreement for your company. Sometimes those terms include the price, sometimes the duration, but ultimately, there are always portions that are essential. Find these provisions and silo them off in your mind — there's no negotiation around them, and no strategy that should put them at risk. If you know what's most valuable, you know what you need to secure.

Set Your Goals for the Contract (and the Partnership) Clearly and Succinctly
This is the one place where we have seen the most problems arise: a failure to understand exactly what it is you're looking for and an accompanying failure to actually write that goal down. It may seem redundant, but the reality is that if you have a written statement of exactly what you want to gain out of your existing relationships, you are far less likely to wander off from your goal or make unnecessary concessions.

Trade Secrets, Derivative Uses, and Special Sauce

What is a "proprietary field" in any given dataset? This is an important question. It's axiomatic that data has value both intrinsically and as a matter of its relationships with other data (that's basically the premise of this book). But data also has value in the sense that it reflects the process it took to create it. The value you ascribe to data, in many ways, depends upon how much effort it took to create, and that effort can also include your own trade secrets, like customer lists or algorithms. You can think of a trade secret as your company's "secret sauce," the internal business method, idea, or product that gives you your competitive edge. Client lists, algorithms, customer preferences, or even sales pitch scripts are also trade secrets, and all are protected by law.

Why are these important to protect? Because they reflect the work that a company has put into developing its business methods and products. If there were no way to protect these kinds of investments, the incentives to poaching employees or secrets would be very high, creating economic havoc. So the law recognizes the importance of trade secrets and, importantly, encourages their development.

There are two kinds of trade secrets at stake in these situations. First, the dataset that you have may be a trade secret — either your own or someone else's. To be a trade secret, a dataset merely needs to be created through your efforts, valuable, and kept secret. That broad definition covers an enormous number of potential datasets, and means that you almost certainly have trade secret datasets. The second trade secret you may have is how you analyze, slice, break down, or otherwise make use of those datasets. Consider, for instance, Zillow's Zestimate, which starts with publicly available data (like historical sales records for a given property and comparable sales in the neighborhood), but uses a proprietary formula to calculate a sales price estimate for any given residential property. The underlying data isn't a trade secret, but the Zestimate formula absolutely is, because it meets those three elements described above: created by Zillow, valuable, and kept secret.

So what does this have to do with data legal basics? Quite a bit, actually. If you're trying to form a data partnership and your dataset is based on your own trade secret data or trade secret formula, sharing it means it isn't a secret anymore. By revealing a trade secret (in the absence of an MNDA or other legal protection), you may effectively waive the right to protection because you have broken the third component of our definition: you didn't keep it secret, and now you can't protect that right in the same way, or, in some circumstances, at all.

To avoid that unpleasant outcome, be sure to think carefully about how you have framed your MNDA, or how you intend to make your presentation more generally. You can also make clear that, in the formation of your data partnership, you should consider if and how you want to maintain control over the derivative uses of your data or your formulas. Conversely, if you are obtaining data from another party, you'll want to guarantee your right to derivative use of data.

We'll discuss derivative data elements further in subsequent chapters, but derivative use is, effectively, the outcome of analysis on a dataset. Most of the time, when you perform an analysis on a dataset you are creating a derivative data element, one that may (or may not) be your property. Of course, depending upon how you create this new derivative data element, it may itself qualify as a trade secret. If you don't carefully consider what rights you have to derivative uses of data, you may inadvertently preclude yourself from using derivative data elements or allow someone else to claim them as their own.

Ultimately, the most important point about trade secrets here is that you understand that they exist. Think carefully about what your trade secrets are, and how you plan to protect yours. If you don't, they may not be secret, or yours, for long.

Read Everything Yourself

Once you understand some of the legal basics, it is critical that you take an active role in your contracts and legal decisions. In our experience, the business owners or product managers who stay close to the contract process when building data partnerships ultimately are more successful than the ones who assume their lawyers can handle it on their own. This is because, as well-qualified and intended as their counsel may be, most lawyers are not familiar enough with the sources, processes, calculation, and presentation of data assets to understand the nuances necessary to gain success in a contractual negotiation. Keep close to the process and, with the help and guidance of your counsel, you will be in a better position to begin leveraging your existing and future relationships to access all of the intrinsic and potentially extrinsic data that you have. Just remember these three pieces of advice that are central to the DataSmart Method:

- Don't think that you can use data just because it is related to your business.
- Read all the contracts, and then read them again.
- Use the contracts that you have to your advantage, including by protecting your data assets.

8

Typical Data Partnerships

DATA PARTNERSHIPS FALL INTO patterns based on how they improve the value of data from the partners. We categorize partnerships based on their end goals. In this chapter, we'll list and describe some of the most common forms of data partnership.

As you contemplate forming one of these partnerships, remember to think about how, when, and why you need to protect the data that you're sharing. One of the most important considerations in privacy is the onward transfer of personal information, particularly if it is to another country; the EU actually forbids transferring personal data out of the Union unless certain (rather stringent) criteria are satisfied. If you don't already know what kind of privacy and data security considerations are at play, you need to *before* you start a new partnership.

Improving Data Quality

The most common data partnership structure is an agreement to share data or purchase data to improve data quality. Businesses must work tirelessly to improve data quality in order to improve the effectiveness of decisions based on the data in datasets. Because no platform has perfect data, there is a need to partner with other firms to compare data and, where appropriate, make changes to your own data to improve its quality. This will help you to escape from the "garbage in, garbage out" principle.

Many data businesses that appear to compete with each other are actually partners in an effort to improve data quality. Firms that specialize in large datasets around businesses, sales numbers, employee counts, and other data fields will often share entire databases with each other to allow for a data quality check. These data businesses don't mind partnering on data quality for most of their base fields, because they have differentiated themselves on other, proprietary fields or values. Many data platform companies are astute at different methods, or focus on different areas from their partner/competitors. For example, some firms are excellent at broad, computer-based methods of gathering data at scale, while others might employ a far more human approach to verify data that is otherwise difficult to gather programmatically. Data quality partnerships enable these firms to make use of the best methods across their datasets.

Not all data quality partnerships include financial considerations. To succeed with a partnership without money changing hands, you need rights to the individual data fields that you plan to use to augment or replace fields in your own files. You'll need to identify these fields and get the rights to them. So, if you are negotiating a data partnership to assist with your data quality, be sure to secure the rights to each of the data fields you may end up using. There may also be limitations in the number of fields you can use for quality purposes. If one party wants to prevent a data quality partnership from really being used as a data append relationship (discussed below), that party can contractually limit the number of fields or percentage of fields that can be used by the other party. This prevents one party from copying the entire database of another.

Data quality partnerships often specify data exchanges at one point in time rather than continuously. Once a year or once a quarter, the partners may share a file, after which they must describe the amount of data they used and the procedures in which it was used. The agreement may include cancellation rights to ensure that both parties, on a quarterly basis perhaps, are comfortable with the value they are getting from mashing these two datasets together to improve quality.

Appending Data (Backfill)

Businesses often purchase additional data fields from another vendor to append or augment their own datasets. These deals are almost always for a monetary consideration and are relatively easy to set up. When you share a list of records with a data append partner, you can have that partner match its records to yours. Your partner will then share with you a list of all the appended attributes it may have for each entity and specify what the cost of proceeding with the append would be.

For example, many consumer retail businesses gather the first name, last name, and email address from as many of their customers as they can. They do this through loyalty programs or data collection by friendly customer service representatives at the point of sale. They gather this data because, so often, when patrons pay with a credit card, the merchant receives no real identifying information.

Once a business has this basic information about its customers, the merchant can reach out to a data supplier to sign up for a data append service. The merchant can upload the data it has — the first name, last name, and email address of their customers — and then that merchant will get back from the data supplier a list of all the "matched" records representing customers for which the supplier can append additional data. This data might include the customer's home address, income level, home-ownership history, education level, social influence score, or any of thousands of other data points. These appends can save enormous amounts of time and effort needed to create a meaningful database about a collection of customers, or improve any other anemic dataset in need of augmentation. You can purchase some append services online with a credit card, uploading a file and seeing available samples of appends before purchasing. The value of any append solution varies based upon the quality of the data being appended as well as the freshness or recency of that data.

Developing New Products

It used to be that businesses would do a little market research surrounding a new product concept, arrive at a go or no-go decision, and proceed. Nowadays, companies are creating fake websites and advertisement for new products and then measuring the interest in these fake products before they ever even set to production.[27] The ability to gather and test data in the development of new products has never been better, and building partnerships around these endeavors has become common.

---

27   See Eric Reis, *The Lean Startup: How Today's Entrepreneurs Use Continuous Innovation to Create Radically Successful Businesses* (New York: Crown, 2011).

By partnering with other companies for their data, a business can leverage those companies' client bases or purchase histories for various products and services without having to actually own this information themselves. Take, for example, a company looking to market a new type of low-fat, gluten-free sandwich bread. The market for such goods has expanded quickly as more people shop for gluten-free options, but the firms who create these products may not have much in the way of market demand data.

Firms like this can now purchase or partner with major grocery retailers or deli chains to find out who their customers are and what their purchase habits look like. While any single delicatessen may not yield much insightful information, if you combine transaction histories from the top 1,000 delicatessens in the nation and further combine that with major grocery chain transaction data, you can see some interesting trends. For example, our gluten-free bread manufacturer could partner to access this data and see what the proportion of sales of gluten-free products are out of total sales of similar products in different geographies over the last three years. Because market segmentation and geographic rollout can make or break a product launch, data can help identify the proper local markets and marketing focus for the product release, and specify which markets aren't worth pursuing.

This type of data deal is ideal for barter, rather than purchase. When launching new products, many companies elect to partner with potential resellers of their products, seeking insights in those resellers' data in exchange for giving those resellers exclusive or advance access to the new product. For top delicatessens or grocery chains, the ability to have a product before others is valuable — and worth the trade of retail data — even if it is just for a limited period of time. This type of partnership thinking requires a proactive data team that can help the product development team to identify the necessary data points they need to make smart decisions quickly.

Reporting

Reporting has grown to be a valuable form of data partnership, often negotiated at no cost to either party. This is excellent because most platforms are evolving to make the ingestion and display of third-party reporting metrics easier. A firm with ad-tech, marketing, CRM, social, and financial software packages will gain valuable synergy between these platforms by viewing their data simultaneously. The issue is that your company may require a view or metric in your reports that isn't part of the standard reporting capability or is unavailable without a partnership agreement in place.

For example, businesses are beginning to understand that there are real insights buried in the data generated by their various efforts — they just have to liberate the insights from the raw data and place those insights in an understandable report. Take a small-business owner who wants to compare its Facebook follower growth to its brand page traffic, its Twitter follower growth, its website traffic from Google searches, and its financial transaction history — and to compare that with its human resources data around new employee hires and work schedules. A business owner comparing all of that data over time can look back at each of their employees to see if any particular hire is tied to increases in social traffic or sales — or the opposite. Businesses like bars, nightclubs, and restaurants have long known that the right employees in the right jobs can have an enormous impact on their client base and sales. Now, with reporting data partnerships, it is easier than ever to view that type of data and the further insights it provides.

This sort of reporting need has given rise to reporting platforms designed to ingest feeds, APIs, or even flat file uploads of data from any source to build insightful views of the data. Domo, based in American Fork, Utah, is one such platform. With APIs and connectivity to almost any other platform available, Domo lets customers build custom reporting interfaces and share them company-wide. TapClicks, based in San Jose, California, is another platform that specifically solves reporting across multiple datasets for digital marketing solutions. Domo has been focused on the massive global enterprise, while TapClicks has focused on the smaller, white-labeled dashboard needs of smaller businesses. Both come at the problem differently, but at their heart, these platforms have massive numbers of data partnerships around reporting content so that they can build entire new experiences in reporting metrics.

Some of the data you require is built into these platforms' software already, because these companies have done the lifting of signing data partnership deals with common data providers. Often times, though, you need to bring additional datasets to your reports that these reporting platforms will not have. In these cases, you should include reporting as a key component of your data partnership thinking. If you partner to access additional datasets, you will need to secure rights from your partners to integrate their data into the third-party reporting tools you utilize.

Building Data Co-Ops

Data co-ops, usually focused around marketing insights, have been around for decades. A data co-op is a platform where you can upload your first-party data to then have access to a much larger combined database about customers, segments, or alternative groupings of customer interests and actions. A co-op is a group of companies or organizations pooling their data about their customers or other entities in one shared platform to gain insights. The theory behind co-ops makes sense for companies that aren't necessarily competing head-to-head, where the sharing of transactional or other data about millions of customers can help them better advertise to those customers.

For example, if you sell outdoor camping goods and have 100,000 customer records, the information around those customers is valuable to you, but may also help others who want to target customers that fit into the "active/outdoor" lifestyle segment for other types of products. Those offering RV rentals, guided tours, outdoor excursions, kayaking, rock climbing, or kite surfing products and services will all be interested in sharing their data with the co-op in exchange for the ability to also see your data about these customers.

Co-ops were much more common in the past. There are still a lot of data partnership opportunities based on the concept today, but the community data approach and central administration are becoming less important as platforms and systems adopt more open API standards. Also, a co-op is only as good as the data in it, which causes a bit of a chicken-and-egg problem. If your data is deep and accurate, does it make sense to contribute to an open forum that others can share? Sometimes you need a laser focus driven by the very highest quality data, rather than the scattershot approach of using many commingled datasets of variable or unknown quality.

While pooled data sounds like an ideal solution, without a robust data compilation process that accurately combines the best aspects of the various datasets, the actual results can be less than stellar. Co-ops and similar solutions suggest that they can accurately combine dataset after dataset in a process where the data improves with each new addition of data. Unfortunately, this tends to not be the case. If you have any dataset, with inherent flaws, and you combine that with another dataset with inherent flaws, you are likely to corrupt more records than you clean or correct. Multiply that concept by 10 or 100 or 1,000 different datasets and you see the problem. Without a thorough, evolving approach to choosing how to combine, clean, merge, match, and append records, co-ops can generate a messy outcome. This tends to be the major drawback of the concept.

Another concern with pooled data is the complicated tasks associated with command, control, and compliance. Sharing resources is a great way to reduce costs and maximize efficiency, but you should also consider how and why you may need to exercise exclusive control over data or, at the very least, how the group will share obligations related to it. What if, for instance, a data subject (like a customer of one of the companies contributing data) asks to access, modify, or delete the data in the shared pool? Who will be responsible for fulfilling that request, modifying the dataset, or deleting the information? And who will bear the legal accountability with regard to the data subject or regulators if something goes wrong? You need to ask these questions at the outset. Like any mutually used resource, data pools present major collective action problems that you must anticipate as best you can from the outset to avoid major complications later.

One bright spot in all of this is that the advancements in AI and machine learning (ML) are drastically improving the process of combining datasets. Because these systems require not only inputs but also outcomes in order to "learn," the future is for every user of the co-op to return values back to the platform, indicating where successful use or failure occurred. Co-ops have the scale necessary for ML applications to iterate to find better outcomes and combinations of datasets. A better outcome might be higher campaign engagement of a particular segment of the data in the co-op or in the successful marketing of overlapping products to a group identified by the co-op as optimally suited to purchase two products together. This requires feedback loops from the company members of the co-op tying outcomes to the data usage. From there, the compilation engine can continuously fine-tune its process. While advancements in AI and ML are promising when dealing with massive datasets like those found in a co-op, this doesn't necessarily mean a data partnership with a co-op is ideal for your use case. We recommend that you test with very specific objectives when exploring this type of partnership. Outline exactly the data or audiences or segments that the co-op is likely to have additional data for and build a test of significant size to verify the results. Asking to run this type of evaluation is standard operating procedure and well worth the effort.

Creating Derivative Data

When you create a new dataset from related data sources to serve a new purpose or create new value, you have created a derivative-use dataset (or just a "derivative dataset"). As we discussed in the previous chapter, this process takes any source data, whether yours or a third party's, and enhances it to serve a new purpose or add value by combining, performing calculations on, reducing, expanding, or in some other way altering the data.

When building data partnerships, many firms have forgotten the most important task in creating derivative works, which is to ensure that your company has the legal rights to derived data. For example, if you want to analyze the average dietary intake of pasta by Americans on a monthly basis, you have many different suppliers of source files with which you could partner to try to derive that data. One such approach would be to go to Yelp, TripAdvisor, or any similar reviews platform and purchase or partner to access a feed of all of their review data about restaurants across the desired geography. From here, using a simple natural language processing approach, you could quickly take the entire dictionary and slang terms for pasta in any form (*spaghetti*, *ziti*, and *mac&cheese*, for example) and extract from the millions of textual reviews of restaurants a compilation of the interest in or mentions of these different pasta types. You could also time-stamp these mentions with the date of the review's creation and build a dynamic time-series view of all pasta types, their popularity, and growth or decline in the United States.

Unfortunately, everything you just did to create the dataset for tracking pasta in the United States is a derivative work based off of the reviews dataset, which is wholly the property of the source from which you got it. Therefore, you would need a contract with the reviews platform that allows for the creation of derivative works from their data, which can be difficult to negotiate. You would need to examine and understand monetary considerations, rights of use, rights of distribution, and a few dozen other legal and structural elements. Some data partners will allow you to create and even sell derivative works, but only so long as you have a current data partnership with their firm as a source of the data. This means that once the contract terminates or expires and you end your partnership, those data partners expect all of your derivative works to remove their valuable data from your dataset. This can prove to be exceedingly difficult, especially if you are combining, as in this example, review data from several platforms with other sources like transactional data from grocery stores.

While negotiating derivative data rights may take considerable effort, there are definite advantages to doing so upfront. Unfortunately, many data companies, especially in their infancy, tend to skip this process and begin building their datasets, deriving them from sources for which they don't have the rights to the data. Case in point: Yelp has for years had to fight off smaller companies that, through data crawlers and scrapers, have been copying reviews and content from Yelp in violation of Yelp's terms and conditions. These companies then sell this data or tools around the data, essentially creating derivative works and services based off of data they don't own. These types of legal battles can be fierce and usually end poorly for those who take source data without the rights and valid data partnerships in place.

This is a very shortsighted approach by the smaller companies that are building a data business. Many forward-thinking companies are quite happy to allow smaller data companies and start-ups access to their data assets with all appropriate rights. The reason for this is simple. With most large organizations, there is only so much time to find new value in their own data. Executives who recognize this lack of focus are open to allowing smaller companies the ability to work on identifying, extracting, and monetizing derivative works. By doing so, the larger organization ensures that their data, which is the source of the new valuable dataset, increases in its attractiveness and usefulness to the market.

IBM, Yelp, Google, Thomson Reuters, First Data, and Equifax are just some of the large companies who specifically set up programs to foster the use of their data by smaller companies to create valuable new derivatives. Naturally, there are some restrictions, usually including the data supplier's right to acquire the company creating the derivative data business, or a right of first refusal regarding such acquisitions. But for many building derivative data products, these constraints are not necessarily showstoppers. We will discuss these types of partnerships and their structures in later chapters. While Rear Admiral Grace Hopper may have said, "It is often easier to ask for forgiveness than to ask for permission," that's a poor strategy if permission is readily available.

Controlling Data

There is an unconventional data partnership structure based around controlling the data that others have about you. Remember, most businesses gather datasets from their operations. However, each record of those datasets usually references one particular entity, like a person or a business or a product. There exists an entire partnership structure in which the entities that this data refers to control or even influence the records that are in these platforms.

Take, for example, your own personal credit report. The credit report for individuals is derived from many different data sources and then aggregated and scored, using different methodologies at each credit reporting agency. For this reason, there is an enormous amount of data about you, but fundamentally, you don't control this data, nor can you block its effect upon your life. That effect, in the case of credit reporting, is substantial.

A couple decades ago, the credit agencies themselves began to open up this content to monitoring. Immediately, new data companies arose that would allow you to monitor or be alerted to the data inside these platforms and what that data said about you. The personal credit monitoring industry is now a multibillion-dollar industry, but what exactly are they selling? It's not the monitoring that is being sold, because that, by itself, does little to help the individual whose credit rating is being harmed by mistakes on their credit report. Instead, they are selling the ability to request changes or fix errors on these data records held by the major credit agencies.

Another such business exists for businesses to control or influence all of the data available about their company or business locations. Firms like Yext, Google, Yelp, and TripAdvisor have businesses or segments that sell the ability to clean up bad data about a business, its locations, products, biographies, or any other attribute of data about them. Companies either pay for this access to clean and manage the data or they agree to broader terms and conditions as the verified owner of the business.

The reason control over content and information about a person or a business is so important is that errors in this information can have substantial negative effects. A business whose retail store locations are incorrect on a map or in local search engines may lose substantial retail revenue. For an interesting demonstration of this, open up Google search in an incognito browser window and type "why did my business" into the search bar. Google, through its massive auto-suggestion platform, will suggest four or more possible searches you are likely to be looking for based on what you've typed in. These are the most common suggestions across trillions of searches, keywords, and results. By the time you type the letter *i* in the word *business*, you will see these top two suggestions:

- "why did my business fail"
- "why did my business disappear from google maps"

This means that of all the questions you might be asking, Google thinks the two most likely are why your business failed or why your business disappeared from Google Maps. The suggestions below the search box are called Google Suggest, which is powered by a number of factors, including the volume of searches for a particular phrase, as well as how many times users interact with that phrase (meaning they select it) among the other phrase options. These two suggestions are first and second on the list, and have been for years, regardless of geographic location — another factor that influences suggested search query terms. While we don't know the exact formula for Google's calculation, the world appears to search for these two queries more than all other questions beginning with "why did my business…"

Sadly, the same can be said for those who have been victims of identity theft or faulty credit reporting in their personal lives. For these people, the horrifying discovery of a terrible personal credit rating usually comes at the most inopportune time, when they are making a life decision around the purchase of a home or a marriage proposal. The immense personal value placed upon credit ratings requires a proactive approach where people can pay for access to these records and the ability to correct them.

Allowing data subjects the right to participate in cleaning up their records (either through a purchased license or, increasingly, as an apology for a breach) is a new approach in data partnership strategies. There are benefits to all involved with these partnerships: the data company will improve their quality with first-party data direct from the person or the company to which each record refers, even as that individual or company benefits from accurate data about them. Expect to see more of these types of services evolve in the future, with more and more industries embracing this process and partnership type.

The concept of controlling data is expanding significantly with the introduction of the GDPR, which went into effect in Europe in May 2018. The GDPR, while focused on privacy issues, also incorporates significant levels of control for individuals. It specifically outlines that individual "data subjects" have the ability to ask any company aggregating, controlling, or processing personal data records about them to provide details on what types and categories of data the company has about them. From there, the individual data subject can ask for the removal of that data (sometimes called "the right to be forgotten") or the ability to correct information.

Although the GDPR is focused on businesses operating in or marketing to Europe, the concept of individuals having more control over the data gathered about them is now a legal responsibility of any company with access to that data. We will dive deeper into data privacy regulations like the GDPR and the deluge of new individual codes being introduced to give greater control to individuals in chapter 12.

Financial Research and Modeling

Financial analysis for investment purposes has long been one of the most active data partnership types. Hedge funds, money management firms, and investment banks spend billions of dollars a year for access to data for analysis. The best and brightest minds in data have often begun their careers in this industry because it is such a fertile and lucrative ground to experiment in, with access to the datasets and tools that build an understanding of the value of data. After all, if you can identify a new data source or derive a new data insight from various other sources of information in an investment setting, then you can potentially turn a profit from the data. This differs from partnerships around developing new products or improving data quality in that the actual goal of the data analysis is to identify investment opportunities, good or bad, and to then commit capital in a manner to arbitrage that informational value.

Most companies that have data assets of any unique value or scale will eventually create a financial industry product offering. Companies like Facebook, Foursquare, and Twitter may not immediately seem like big data providers to Wall Street, but they absolutely are. Each of those companies has divisions and teams dedicated to the structure and sale of their data to companies for the purpose of financial research and modeling. Many of these companies refer to this type of content as "alternative research" sources, meaning they are alternatives to the typical investment data from accounting statements, economic reports, revenue forecasts, and same-store sales figures.

You should consider this market from a data partnership strategy perspective when building out a data plan. Many companies in manufacturing, delivery, logistics, insurance, satellite imagery, retail, and online traffic measurement have funded their data products and services growth by building a small financial services team. This market values unique datasets. Even if you have only a few investment managers as clients, they will often pay for exclusivity or limited distribution controls to ensure that their investment shop gains an edge.

Financial research partnerships require that you provide them with legal rights of use necessary for them to build derivative datasets. Investment firms must have confidence that the data comes with the necessary permissions. Because investment firms may ultimately commit significant capital to the ideas or information derived from your data and other sources, they will expect to have their rights clearly established in writing, and will not hesitate to enforce those rights. If your firm decides to build out financial research and investment firm data partnerships, you should work to prepare all of the disclosures and legal outlines that explain the sources of your data and the types of data you will be providing. This will greatly streamline any efforts to build a market in this vertical.

Reselling Partnerships

Reseller agreements and affiliate agreements are an increasingly common structure in data partnership strategy. The defining difference in these partnerships is that the partner receiving the data resells it to generate revenue. Reseller partnerships can return value by returning lead referrals to your company or reward you with a proportion of their revenue from selling your data, perhaps in conjunction with data from others. The number of structures is as varied as the data being sold, but there are some simple commonalities. We explain more about these types of partnerships in chapter 11.

Reselling partnerships are built with the concept that whichever company is selling the data to the ultimate data buyer will own and manage the relationship. The reseller is responsible for the end data buyer's experience, including invoicing and contracts. The reseller will pay you a wholesale rate to provide your data to their buyer.

Affiliate partners, on the other hand, introduce leads to your company and are paid a commission for introductions that become paying customers. In an affiliate relationship, you will control the relationship with the data buyer, invoicing, and contracts, and the affiliate partner is really only obligated to accurately represent your dataset to potential customers. While there are hybrid flavors of these types of partnerships, the vast majority fall into one of these two structures.

Many data companies exist as "data marts" where a marketplace of different data assets reside. These companies are typically combinations of affiliate and reseller deals, depending upon how big the data mart is and what their customer relationships are built upon. For example, Bloomberg in the financial services industry may appear to be a highly sophisticated technology platform (which it is), but at its core, the Bloomberg terminal is a box filled with thousands of data partnerships, some affiliate, some reseller. When logging into a Bloomberg terminal, you receive access to a vast library of data, from market information to international football scores in real time. Bloomberg is reselling this data to you, based on their data partnerships. Other sources of content on these terminals, like Wall Street investment bank research reports, are typically available through an affiliate deal where a complex authentication and permissioning system on the Bloomberg terminal keeps track of who can access that data and when. To access these custom reports or proprietary datasets, the customer must have a direct contract and financial arrangement with the Wall Street investment bank, which then logs into the Bloomberg permission-based system to "grant access" to their data for that particular customer.

These platforms, like Bloomberg, have built up superior client relationships and capabilities by making it easier for data providers to access the financial services market. Often, data providers can't (and probably shouldn't) compete with these platforms. Instead, they can tap them to gain rapid and protected exposure to an industry. Salesforce's cloud community of applications and datasets is another outstanding example of a partnership ecosystem enabling customers, whether through resale or affiliate contracts, to access data where they need it, reducing friction and increasing adoption speed.

Target Marketing

Marketers favor another partnership type: the sharing and use of data to refine their reach and efficacy. Improving targeting in the advertising and marketing of products and services has been an area of immense growth in the past 20 years.

Target data seeks to resolve the age-old problem immortalized by John Wanamaker: "Half the money I spend on advertising is wasted; the trouble is I don't know which half." Digital marketing tools and datasets can improve companies' marketing spend and offer some better insight into the common attributes of their current customers. Target marketing approaches demand a thorough understanding of current customers. You can use data partnerships to quickly find out what a typical customer looks like.

Digital marketing companies can quickly analyze attributes including your customers' income, geography, interests, social network participation, reading habits, careers, and past purchases. Think of each of these data points as an adjective describing your current customer base. If you share or upload a list of your 100 best customers, these digital marketing data machines can suggest that you market to a whole new list of customers that share key attributes with your best customers. This process is called "customer cloning" or "look-alike" modeling and basically identifies all of the key attributes that make up your best customers.

Another approach to targeting uses digital browsing history to target or "retarget" those who have shown some element of interest in your products or services in the past. This is why those shoes you looked at on Cole Haan's website seem to follow you around the internet no matter where you go. Retargeting has a high "creepy" factor for many internet users because, as with all good marketing tactics, practitioners have overused it and made it very obvious that they are following your every move. Publishers and social media sites use browser cookies to enable retargeting. They know which sites the browser has visited, what the user clicked on, even how far into the sales funnel the consumer may have descended before abandoning their shopping cart. Many of these platforms also track dwell time, which lets them know just how long you might have been staring at those Cole Haan shoes before deciding that today wasn't the day to buy them. Marketers can leverage these factors in creative ways to increase the efficacy of their targeting. Retargeting works really well, but marketers must balance it with privacy issues and the danger of being perceived as creepy.

These days, geolocation and time are the basis for the most sought-after target marketing partnerships. Knowing where a person is at a particular time is of immense target marketing value. Because most consumers have many different personas throughout the day, their location and time can significantly enhance how marketers reach out to them. For example, when someone is commuting into New York City in the morning, advertising a lunch special in their hometown is less than optimal. Not only is the intended customer not currently near their hometown, but they are, in fact, headed in the opposite direction. Using location, direction, and time, marketers are beginning to target individuals in the moment with much more appropriate messaging. As we mentioned earlier, this has evolved into "conquesting," and includes using GPS signals to enable messaging people as they pull into a competitor's parking lot, or offering a discount or incentive for the consumer to exit that parking lot and head on over to the competitor for a better deal. Conquesting has taken off, but is only possible through partnerships with apps or other location-service-enabled platforms.

For all of these partnership types, you must identify what types of data will really add benefit to your targeting. Fortunately, regardless of whether you are the supplier or user of data for marketing purposes, you can quickly and efficiently test the data and observe lift or the lack thereof. By working with a beta partnership agreement or a smaller sample dataset, you can analyze how well the new data did at improved marketing outcomes.

Summarizing Typical Data Structures

If you focus on the desired use or outcomes of any data partnership, the right structure will begin to unfold. If you need derivative rights or reseller rights or just want to increase your marketing campaign conversion rates, each of those needs will help define your preferred deal structure. We expect geolocation, identity suppression, and artificial intelligence to rapidly become new data partnership use cases, but for now they are still relatively new.

In the next several chapters we will take these structures and place them into specific contexts with specific partner types on both sides of the table. You will be able to take advantage of this provided that you have identified your data assets, assigned a value to them, and recognized common structures you can use to build partnerships.

9

The Innovator Data Partnership

I N T H E   N E X T   F E W chapters we will examine some of the most common data partnership combinations. Datasets, their value, and their
value in partnerships are infinitely variable. To provide some insight into
that variety, we'll examine some of the most common partnerships from
the perspective of the partner who owns or controls the data, starting with
the innovator data partnership.

An innovator data partnership starts with an innovative, nimble firm,
typically a smaller company, seeking to create a new partnership to
leverage the data they create. These partnerships focus on the promise
of business opportunities for new uses of data. Each party in this relationship has different needs depending upon who controls the source of
the data.

The meetings that lead to innovator partnerships are both exciting and
frustrating. Because there are few precedents, it's difficult to agree on a
value for innovators' unique data. For example, when search engine optimization platforms first began to emerge, their creators quickly found
that while the meetings with potential partners were promising, many
lacked the capability to effectively capitalize on the keyword, traffic, and
trending data. Sometimes, innovator data appears as a solution in search
of a problem. To drive these partnerships, you need good timing and
an internal champion for the value of the data at one or both parties to
the partnership.

We'll analyze these partnerships from two perspectives: when the
innovator is the source of the data, and when the innovator is seeking data
from another platform to build something new.

When the Innovator Is the Source of the Data

As companies emerge with new datasets, they quickly begin to realize that their information may be more valuable in the hands of other companies. The Weather Channel realized this truth decades ago as it began to market its weather data to other companies, at first just to augment news, television, and radio websites with upcoming forecasts. Commodity traders, hedge funds, advertisers, and a myriad of additional buyers were soon lining up to access the dataset. It took a dedicated team of data partnership professionals to build the value proposition for this data in the market. Once this team established the impact of weather on different sectors and industries, the momentum began to shift in their favor.

Most companies that are a source of new or innovative data, lacking the resources to exploit it fully, need help from larger companies or those with broader distribution to help them monetize their data. Large data or information service companies typically have teams that find these new data sources and negotiate with them. These teams used to wear the title of "business development" but have evolved to focus more specifically on data origination and partnership.

What does a data innovator need to succeed? Distribution, champions, reporting, data protection, and promotion. Let's examine each of these needs in detail.

Distribution and Sales
As we've explained, innovative data companies have a dataset, a product, or both with unique capabilities. They also typically have intellectual property or trade secrets to protect their derivative or calculated data. When they approach a larger company (which, in this chapter, we'll be calling the "data platform"), they are likely seeking a partnership around the sale and distribution of their data. The structure of these partnerships can range from selling data into a "data marketplace" to a more integrated experience between the two companies.

When a data innovator approaches a Bloomberg, Thomson Reuters, FactSet, Acxiom, Infogroup, Pitney Bowes, or any of hundreds of other data platforms, it must stay focused on the objective. If a dataset is truly innovative, the terms of its proposed distribution deal may be difficult to swallow. As a data innovator, you'll encounter demands for large percentages of revenue, strict terms surrounding what constitutes a sale or introduction made by the larger company, and a right of first refusal.

You have to prioritize your responses. Focus on the ongoing revenue share and terms of renewal. Place limits not just on the scope of revenue share but also on the timeframe. Try to limit the scope of revenue share to only the data actually delivered through or by the larger distribution company or platform. In other words, if you empower the larger firm to sell a finite type of data or subset, you should not need to share revenue on additional datasets or deeper service levels to the customers they bring you. Renewal terms should allow renegotiation of revenue share amounts. It is great when these relationships work out, but in case the larger sales organization providing distribution adds no ongoing value at renewal or in the years beyond the first introduction, renewal terms should not remain the same or become less favorable for the data innovator.

Despite the challenges, there are real benefits to this type of relationship, because proper distribution can accelerate the data innovator's exposure and revenues. Many data platforms combine established data with a unique dataset to improve its value. Weather data combined with financial data on stocks, through time and across geographies, is more valuable than weather data alone. Product adoption data is more valuable when integrated with social data feeds. Customer segmentation data is more valuable when integrated directly with content engagement data. There is great value in the mere proximity of a newer data company's data products to more established datasets delivered through a globally recognized data exchange. This is why the larger data platform company's distribution can legitimately ask for, and receive, highly favorable terms.

To be fair to the larger data platform companies, there is a good reason they seek favorable terms from smaller data innovators. If a global data platform is able to recognize the value of your data, and then help you distribute and sell that data to their clients and prospects, they are increasing the value of your company. You must pay for that increase in enterprise value by sharing significant portions of the revenue or offering the platform favorable terms should they seek an acquisition. Don't allow yourself to be forced into an overly restrictive or exclusive arrangement when flexibility and scalability are what you need most.

There are a couple of ways to handle this from the innovator's perspective. First, if you can segment, refine, or alter the dataset to make it unique for each different reseller platform, you may be able to strike more favorable terms while maintaining more control. To use an example from market investment research, if one platform has the rights to resell historical data, while another platform has the right to sell only forecast data (forward-looking), you can get more favorable terms from each. By presenting some unique form of your innovative data to each partner, you can maintain more control by limiting the distribution.

Another way to handle this challenge is to rapidly line up several different data partnership platform negotiations at the same time. By pitting the larger firms against each other, you make them compete for access to resell your data to their audience. Negotiate specific marketing activities to be contractually provided by the data platform. For example, insist on webinars, email marketing campaigns, website ads, platform ratings or recommendations, and bundled offers. If you press for bundled offers, the resulting distribution deal requires the reseller or distributor to include your innovative data asset as part of their offering. In this way, as they sell their platform to customers, your cost is bundled into their cost, usually to the tune of a guaranteed amount of revenue. This type of guaranteed revenue is a great way to build the revenue stream for a small company.

Internal Champions

In nearly every deal between a data innovator and a larger platform, someone at the platform company is an internal champion for the deal.

With new datasets and innovative data, the process of educating a potential partner can be very difficult. Someone needs to spell out the value proposition repeatedly, explaining it to each successive decision-maker. An internal champion at the platform company can dramatically improve this frustrating and demoralizing process. The champion guides your efforts and your pitch. They are the critical access point to the right decision-makers.

At most large platform companies, internal champions are in business development and strategy departments. Many larger companies also now have "data partnership" teams whose mission is to identify new datasets. Like business development people, these teams are a great starting point for the introduction and dissemination of information throughout the organization, but don't typically have all of the necessary momentum to create urgency. The secret to working with these teams is to leverage them as your first internal champion, who will then lead you to the next champion in the revenue or sales organization.

To move the deal forward, you'll need to find the internal champion in the revenue organization at a major platform company. Revenue, sales, and marketing all need to see the value and opportunity in your dataset. Remember, these departments are paid on sales and typically don't care what your revenue split is within the data partnership contract. This means you must work with sales leadership to explain the unique value your data can provide and help train their teams for success. Once you find this champion in the revenue organization, you will see substantially higher urgency and interest from the data partnership team or the business development team.

Lastly, it is your job, and your team's job, to collectively empower the champions at every partner. Too many innovative data companies assume that everyone can see the genius in their concept or dataset, which is never the case. Building case studies, gathering testimonials, and building a comprehensive and solid data catalog (as discussed in chapter 6) will empower your champions properly. They need ongoing support to ensure that your data product continues to receive the attention it deserves.

User Growth and Reporting
Data innovators need access to rapid user growth and reporting metrics from their platform partners. This helps those innovative data suppliers to learn how best to market, sell, and support new partners, based on how existing platform users are using the suppliers' data. Each sector and industry may approach their new dataset from a different value perspective; political organizations have different needs from financial investment firms.

For this reason, it is vital in an innovator data partnership for the smaller firm, the source of the data, to gain access to user metrics and reporting from platform partners. The insights from this data are critical as they seek to grow their business and build out their products. The contract between the companies should describe reporting requirements, including an outline of the fields that will be provided to the data supplier. Ideally, the platform company should provide a reporting API that shows usage over different timeframes. The data supplier can justify this reporting as the benchmark by which both parties will value the relationship going forward.

Because of the GDPR in Europe and various resolutions or laws in the United States affecting data sharing, consider privacy when requesting usage data and reporting. The more personal data you have, the more obligations you have to protect it. For that reason, it's often better to request anonymized or aggregated data measures from your platform partner rather than full access to names, company employees, and email addresses. Increasingly, access to that level of personally identifiable information carries significant risks and generates additional privacy requirements.

To cut back on those risks, you can limit usage data, client access, and customer identities to company names or even aggregate measures across sectors, industries, or client types. It may be enough for a smaller data innovator to receive daily or weekly reports that outline the total number of views, downloads, or app requests from a larger platform distributor. Have a very clear understanding of what data you need, or what data your partner needs, for the use cases you've outlined or the value proposition you set up. If a dataset contains personal data that doesn't serve those purposes, don't acquire it. Knowing what features are working, which datasets are most interesting, and which data points are selling the fastest may be far more important to the long-term success of your data sales than the actual identity of each person accessing the data.

Permissions and Protection of the Data Assets
Most data platform providers have highly sophisticated permissioning systems that regulate users' access to content. Think of these systems as gatekeeping tools that identify which customers have access to your innovative new dataset and which customers haven't yet paid for the data. Throw in "trial periods," special offers, bundles, and cancellations, and you will begin to see a massively complex architecture designed to protect both your data and the overall platform itself. Just as your cable television or internet package has hundreds of different packages for premium

channels, sports, international, children's programming, and triple-play packages for phone, internet, and television, your data distribution partner's platforms are similarly complex.

The good news is that these platforms tend to offer a lot of flexibility. As the smaller, innovative firm, before you sign the contract, it really pays to get to know the permissioning platform well. If you have an excellent understanding of partners' permissioning and protection philosophy, you can build specific requests into the contract to ensure more successful adoption by the sales and account management teams. We've unfortunately made the mistake of doing this wrong in the past, in a case where a data partner's content was truly outstanding, but less than ideal packaging and permissioning and bad categorization inhibited discoverability of the data. This eventually diffused any excitement the sales team felt about introducing the dataset to their clients, because the data wasn't easy to discover and appeared to pertain to construction costs when it was actually about real estate pricing. Understand the way the gatekeeper software works and optimize carefully how customers will gain access to your data. Internal champions can help with this.

Go beyond the permissioning system and include usage reporting and auditing rights in your contract. Beyond the reporting data described in the previous section, you need data audit rights to verify that your distribution partner is living up to its end of the deal. Unfortunately, the more complex it is to access your data on the platform — for example, as a part of a bundled dataset — the more complex it is to track usage and access. Additionally, you'll want access to the documentation at these firms that describes employee access and usage. Too many contracts essentially ignore this concern, or worse, they grant full access rights for the platform's employees or operations personnel so as to give them an umbrella of protection to operate however they deem appropriate. Avoid this leaky bucket. Understanding what can be accessed, by whom, and for what purpose is a critical add to any data partnership deal.

In this new world of data privacy and compliance, it is easy to see how Facebook's data sharing protocols, which were themselves apparently legal, caused problems when that data was subsequently provided to unauthorized users for unauthorized purposes. Make sure your contracts with larger distribution platforms don't suffer from this lack of clarity.

Promotion

Don't overlook promotion as a negotiating point in the contract. It is too easy to get caught up in the potential of a major data partnership without recognizing that promotion details can make or break it.

Large sales and marketing platforms with seemingly limitless distribution will often make promises that stretch beyond their ability to deliver. Remember, every dataset under the sun is trying to leverage these platforms and app markets to connect them to potential users. The result is often disappointing. In the beginning of 2018 there were over 2 million different apps in the Apple App Store, and over 3.8 million apps available in the Google Android ecosystem.[28] The reality is that most app markets or large-scale data distribution platforms just can't attract enough downloads of individual datasets to generate significant revenue for smaller innovative companies without proper promotion. Building promotional elements directly into your data partnership agreement is the key to unlocking the potential of these platforms. Without this, you might spend a lot of time on the legal contract and integration effort only to end up in the data partner "graveyard" that every major platform has but doesn't like to admit exists.

From webinars to joint email marketing campaigns, you need to outline specific marketing ideas and include them in the contract. Consider your dataset and the target audience. While a Bloomberg terminal or Thomson Reuters platform has lots of potential user types, you can identify which of those are most appropriate for your dataset and focus promotion on those groups. This could mean focusing on portfolio managers over traders, or research analysts over trading operations managers. Once you have identified the right audience, your requests for promotions in the agreement will appear more reasonable to the larger platform provider.

Ultimately, while larger data distribution providers are certainly interested in having more data on their platforms, they don't have the resources to promote each one effectively. Before signing any form of partnership, work out the promotional materials, cadence, and guaranteed effort that

---

28   "Number of Apps Available in Leading App Stores as of 3rd Quarter 2018," Statistica, October 2018, www.statista.com/statistics/276623 /number-of-apps-available-in-leading-app-stores/.

you both will put into marketing the new dataset. The other obvious benefit to this approach is that the salespeople at the larger platform company will be the first to consume the story about your data and will give you solid feedback on whether they see the pitch delivering or not.

When the Larger Data Platform Is the Source of the Data

Up until this point, we have discussed data partnerships for innovative datasets from the perspective of the smaller firm as the source of the data in the partnership. The reverse is also possible, when the larger data platform company supplies the data. For example, Foursquare and Yelp provide data to smaller innovative companies all the time. Similarly, HERE, the global mapping platform and data provider based in the Netherlands, also has programs to let data innovators build upon their datasets. Each of these firms have significant global data assets, particularly as it pertains to local, map, and business data, and they have built successful partnership strategies to empower smaller companies with their data assets.

Larger firms with substantial capabilities in either data or platform have long recognized that if they opened up access to their more commoditized datasets, they could create a digital playground for entrepreneurs. They may never let their large competitors access the information, but letting smaller data innovators who have an interesting point of view, or perhaps a derivative dataset in mind, can often generate innovation at scale. They typically expose both the datasets and the functionality through APIs. Each innovative company seeking to build derivative datasets either accepts general terms and conditions of programmatic access or they sign a simple data and API access agreement that stipulates how and for what purpose they can use the data of the larger platform company. Then the lab experiments begin, where further opportunities present themselves.

Access to Innovation
The first opportunity for larger platform companies in allowing data innovators to access their data is access. When these innovators build new products, solutions, or capabilities, the data platform can have a "first look" at those innovators' new approaches to leveraging their data. Apple,

Google, Amazon, Facebook, Yelp, Foursquare, Salesforce, Adobe, Yext, and hundreds of companies use this approach to unlock innovation by creating an efficient playground for others to access and leverage their datasets and capabilities.

When you control access to a dataset that stands out for its size or quality, you have the opportunity to empower thousands, or hundreds of thousands, of developers and engineers to build new toys. Your current operations generate the raw materials but can't possibly scale internal development to chase all the possibilities. The solution is opening up a data partnership program to outside developers, effectively encouraging them.

Often, third parties seeking access to your data are also expecting to create a more valuable derivative dataset. From the larger platform's perspective this has the added benefit of coupling innovation with access to innovative founders and developers. An open framework allows companies to develop valuable relationships with these creators of derivative data, tools, and services. It all starts with access to brilliant teams seeking to take your data to the next level.

Variety and Reinvention

By providing access, large platform businesses that supply data to smaller innovators create variety across their platform. The varied solutions within the large platform company's ecosystems are a selling point to the platform's own client base. When customers are considering a data platform purchase, they often demand this type of variety. Integrations, partnerships, and reporting solutions across dozens, hundreds, or even millions of additional applications is a strong selling point.

Variety also brings with it the benefit of selection. A highly adaptable group of data partners, constantly evolving and competing, generates more quality derivative data services. The variety creates competition across sales, account management, and operations and can help the platform to identify which opportunities are ready for acquisition or exclusivity. For large data providers, variety opens up opportunities to find the next big thing, because customer interaction across a large, differentiated ecosystem drives innovation.

For platforms seeking to build out their app ecosystem or their app marketplace, variety is also a necessity. Larger data platforms in the beginning stages of launching their app market or integrated solutions need to attract developers. Providing data and tools for free or for reduced or deferred payment can be an excellent bargaining chip to attract new development partners and innovation. There is risk, though. Many smaller, innovative platform players have experience with large firms and are quite accustomed to identifying weaknesses and opportunities in a new ecosystem.

Variety also offers the benefit of reinvention. Depending upon the contract, many large data platforms have the right or opportunity to enter the same market as the smaller innovative firms. It may seem unfair, but realistically, many of these contracts contain a detailed provision that expressly states that the data platform, or source of the data, is not precluded from entering the same market as the smaller, innovative partner firm. We've seen this happen over the years, time and time again: a large platform eventually jettisons a younger upstart and then launches a substantially similar solution. Sometimes this occurs following a failed acquisition attempt, but more often than not, it is just the result of a contract that permits it and an opportunity that the larger partner can't ignore.

A note for the smaller, innovator partner here: you can protect yourself from this scenario by safeguarding your intellectual property. Apply for a patent or build a client base that can help protect your data solution. Or, perhaps better, ensure that you choose data partners and platforms that don't have a reputation for idea "farming" from their smaller partnerships.

Branding, Attribution, and Exclusivity

Larger data platforms that supply source data to innovative firms can demand attribution and branding rights. Requiring data partners to disclose on their site or in their terms and disclaimers that the platform is the source of a particular source of data will immediately return benefits. Attribution can also help larger platforms attract additional innovative companies to their platform by publicizing that they are powering other similar companies.

When Apple Maps was building out its map platform, the news media closely followed all of the sources of data that it listed in its terms and conditions. It was a badge of honor for many data companies to have passed the Apple Maps test and to have made it into Apple's dataset, and subsequently, to millions of iPhone users. Apple uses this attribution, this badge of honor, to their benefit. They attract great datasets and partnership terms in exchange for allowing others to be affiliated with their logo or brand. Like Amazon and Google, Apple also does not allow businesses to associate themselves with their brand without express written permission. These behemoths defend their brands zealously; for a small, innovative application or dataset creator to be affiliated with one of these brands is a testament to their data worth.

Exclusivity is a close relative of attribution and branding. For many top-tier data platforms or resellers, the ability to negotiate exclusive access to certain datasets, whether original or derivative, is an intelligent approach to increasing their value proposition. Data innovators should avoid licensing exclusivity, even as large data platforms seek it. A large platform with the ability to secure exclusive datasets through sharing access and use of the platform's data assets can be dangerous. For many smaller companies, you need to evaluate closely whether or not an exclusive arrangement is really worth limiting your distribution. Exclusive distribution rights may make more sense if there are also reciprocal exclusive rights preventing the large platform from partnering with any competing solutions to the data innovator's approach.

Other Rights and Controls

For the large data platform supplying datasets to a partnership, there is always the concern that the smaller firm will eventually provide what it is creating to a competitor. This is a common issue with the development of new, more open data architectures. In truth, large data platforms that provide data typically don't need to worry about small, innovative players. Instead, what they need are rights of first refusal to acquire these smaller firms.

While these rights are desirable for large platforms, deciding whether to grant that right of first refusal is a complicated task for data innovators. For these companies, the data provided by the platform provider will need to be unique and of such a great value to the innovator's own dataset that no substitution could really replace it. This is unlikely in today's world, where many datasets are in a race to commoditization, rather than surrounded by a moat of invincibility. Large platforms will need to continue to add real value to the partnership, because data innovators have little incentive to limit their distribution or capitalization options in exchange for the same old data they can secure elsewhere.

As discussed above, the marketing and promotion of new datasets and partnerships is vitally important to small firms to ensure their capabilities are discoverable within a large platform. Conversely, large platforms benefit from promoting innovation and new capabilities. Because they typically hold more of the power in the relationship, large platforms should insist on maintaining control over press releases, marketing materials, sales collateral, and even training materials. When you are Apple, Amazon, Facebook, Google, or any other global platform, proximity to your brand is a huge benefit for smaller, innovative companies. If you are managing the data partnership strategy for a larger platform that contributes data, consider a "trusted" data partner program with its own badge or seal and value proposition. These platforms' contracts will need to require written approval of any materials produced by the smaller firm and they will also need to keep track of these materials. Too many large platforms fight for this contract provision but then do little to police what smaller data partners are saying about them after signing. Brand risk all too often becomes a problem because there wasn't an ongoing strategy to monitor data partners.

Summarizing the Innovator Data Partnership

Innovation in data is constant. Your business can't do it all. The goal in the innovator data partnership is to help data companies, large and small, leverage each other's strengths to build new capabilities and to attack the market faster than they might be able to do on their own. If you are a large data or distributed platform company, immediately create and promote data sharing and innovation markets for smaller companies. If you are a smaller, innovative company, stop worrying about someone stealing your idea or data and find a champion at a large platform company to help scale your data operation and sales.

10

Mutually Beneficial Data Partnerships

T HE MUTUALLY BENEFICIAL DATA partnership may sound like a unicorn, but it is actually quite common. Market forces drive these partnerships for one of three reasons: shared clients, operational teams, and marketing. This contrasts with innovator partnerships, which are driven by sales opportunities, product innovation, and channel distribution.

Mutually beneficial partnerships tend to form between partners of similar size and scope. For this reason, the contracts between these companies are more balanced, with similar rights, indemnities, and considerations for both parties. Many of these partnerships don't require payments between the parties concerned, but they do create cost savings, improve retention, and lower marketing expenses. Only the largest platforms can actually generate additional revenue from mutually beneficial data partnerships by means of their semi-monopolistic control over a particular market or platform.

Customer-Driven Data Partnerships

Every business wants to keep current customers happy. To this end, your product or service has to meet current needs and evolve to meet the future needs of your client base.

When it comes to data partnerships, over the last 10 years there has been a significant increase in "customer-driven" partnerships, in which a client will ask a data provider, platform, or service to integrate its data with data from another platform or service. Clients of your data solution often use multiple platforms. For this reason, they may ask (or demand) that data companies create cross-platform integrations to ensure that they have simpler access to the combined data they need.

The challenge is that customers are beginning to expect this type of integration at little or no cost. Customers may not realize that a proper integration of two datasets can be extremely difficult and time-consuming. Consider foot traffic and sales transactions at a given store location. A business may have foot traffic data from its in-store Wi-Fi provider, and it most certainly has its POS system data, which shows all transactions for a given location, but matching up these two datasets from different providers can be a nightmare. While the time of a transaction, or time of day for foot traffic, can be used to crosswalk from one dataset to another, integration is typically not simple, and a qualified analytics team will need to review the potential insights from making such a leap.

Knowing that this type of data is messy, who gets paid to integrate the two datasets? Who will provide the analytical oversight and review to ensure that the data is being merged and analyzed properly? From your point of view, as a data partnership participant, you must carefully consider the goals, costs, and timelines of such an integration. These projects tend to spin out of control because the customer who originally requests the integration between two data platforms may not have a clear goal in mind. In short, these requests are often "fishing expeditions" to see if an initial theory is valid or not.

For customer-driven data partnerships, demand a clear professional services pricing strategy. Without one, or without a clear mandate of replying "no" to these types of requests, salespeople are often left too much latitude when deciding if an integration is acceptable or not, and how to price it. Because sales staff rarely have to fulfill what they sell, this leads to a natural bias toward agreement with the prospect or customer to expedite the sale, ignoring the costs and complexities.

You can include professional services in a contract simply by describing the details of this type of additional data partnership engagement. By including a professional services fee and structure, your company is ensuring that any customer-driven partnerships will be viewed through the lens of "additional work," which helps you begin negotiation from a discernible initial fee, as opposed to starting with a fee of zero dollars looking to move upward. Ideally, in a mutually beneficial data partnership, the customer should pay the professional services to connect the platforms but will not have exclusivity for the new connected capability. In this way, a data provider can receive payment to extend its platform integrations without taking a loss on the work.

For most data companies, mutually beneficial data partnerships focus on non-competitive datasets. When a customer directs a data platform to partner with another provider or source of data, it is rarely for the same or similar data.

There is one other approach to customer-driven data partnerships. When a smaller, innovative data company supplies data to a large customer, the data supplier should leverage the client's power to press for data partnerships wherever possible. By asking a large client, one with influential reach, to make a request of another data or platform company, you can improve the utility of your data and the overall appeal of your platform or dataset. To your customer, so long as the request is reasonable and the value proposition clear, there is almost no downside in asking. We have seen many smaller data platforms grow through this approach by finding a champion at their larger customers to help drive mutually beneficial partnerships with additional platforms that would be normally considered way out of their league.

Operationally Driven Data Partnerships

Operationally driven data partnerships are all about efficiency. They arguably represent the fastest growing relationships between major platforms, because as companies continue to evolve their own data strategies, there are enormous pressures to keep costs down and efficiency up. Financial services platforms for trading and banking were some of the first to adopt highly efficient integrations with each other for the transaction, settlement, and funding of trades and accounts, but they have very quickly been surpassed by countless marketing and social platforms.

As with customer-driven data partnerships, many of these operational efficiencies are requested by customers; however, many data businesses can recognize the likely market outcome before a customer asks for it. Take, for example, the CardLinx Association. This platform was created to provide seamless loyalty and discount solutions across financial platforms from credit cards to payment processors, marketers, and retailers. Mastercard, TransUnion, First Data, Discover, Bank of America, and Sumitomo Cards, to name just a few of the members of the CardLinx Association, all benefit from the universal need for operational efficiency of integrated systems. Before their alignment on how to track rebates, discounts, loyalty points, and transactions, most major retailers just had stickers or punch cards. Remember those days? Now we live in a world where your loyalty program connects to your credit card, which connects to your discounts and purchase information. This efficiency creates a new opportunity for every partner in the network, and each platform plays an important role.

Another excellent example of operationally driven benefit comes from the fitness data industry. Fitness apps, watches, bands, clips, and heart monitors have been around for a long time. As they have evolved and grown in market share, so too has the volume and depth of the data they collect: heart rate, speed, miles traveled, GPS waypoints, height, weight, and even SWOLF score (yeah, look it up; it's like a golf score for swimming). Users want to transfer and combine that data in multiple formats for further use and analysis.

At first, this data was captive and held hostage in whichever brand or platform you purchased. Your Apple Watch wouldn't share information with your Garmin swim watch, and they surely would never share with your Polar heart rate monitor. For each of these companies, the desire to keep personal health data captive was a business decision meant to drive loyalty and lifetime value from each user. The problem with this approach is that, fundamentally, users viewed this data as their own property and struggled to find ways to migrate and share the data between platforms.

Demand from the consumer to allow their data to be migrated or shared across these platforms started with the Strava App. Strava is a fitness enthusiast's dream, with incredibly detailed analysis about your improvement or decline in almost every aspect of your activity, including just how much deep sleep you got last night. For Strava to work, though, it needed to connect to data from various platforms in an operationally efficient way. Consumers pushed each vendor toward this, and to some degree, just as with CardLinx, the opportunity to deliver a great customer experience outweighed the potential benefits of the hostage data approach. Strava has quickly risen to connect Garmin, Apple, TomTom, Timex, Suunto, Polar, and just about every other fitness tracking platform, and it shows no signs of slowing down.

Two Perspectives on Operationally Driven Data Partnerships

You can view operationally driven data partnerships through the eyes of the data company or platform that is providing the service, or through the perspective of the user, who desires an efficient, non-captive experience.

The data platform's perspective typically favors the captive data approach, in contrast to a more open data framework that shares what could be proprietary data with others. When it comes to operational efficiency, as in the CardLinx Association, the data owners recognized that, although they may compete with each other in some aspects of their businesses, the massive market opportunity of creating a comprehensive solution to this complex financial transaction problem was worth the potential loss of advantage. This same realization drove the New York Stock Exchange, Nasdaq, and other global markets to allow third parties to integrate with their feeds to access real-time stock prices. In both these cases, data originally was captive and then slowly opened up as the market opportunity became clear.

Sometimes data companies and platforms recognize these opportunities themselves, but sometimes market disruptors come along and figure out ingenious ways to access the data they need. This is the concern that many companies now face, with structured data easily scraped or ingested by massive data-crawling platforms. The legality of taking what is visible to any visitor of a website and programmatically gathering and storing that data for use is not yet settled. On one hand, companies can use their terms and conditions to prevent or dissuade such activity, but on the other hand, they let Google and Apple crawl and store their data because of their reliance on those platforms for users to discover them. When it's easy to pull companies' data from their data platforms, disruptors can push those same companies to adopt more operationally efficient approaches to sharing their information. From a data partnership perspective, if your role within your organization is to manage this trade-off, you need to focus on what customers are asking for as well as what data innovators are doing around your data.

The other perspective of operationally driven data partnerships is from the user's or consumer's point of view. Most people want to simplify their lives. Also, humans are lazy. Regardless of whether you ascribe people's behavior to simplification or laziness, most consumers are willing to connect different data platforms to get a better or more efficient experience.

For example, millions of people find it a burden to keep track of their personal banking statements, 401(k) plans, college savings plans, expenditures, and stock portfolios. Unfortunately, since each of those platforms or tools typically become part of a user's life at different times, the solutions tend to come from different companies. Naturally, each of those companies provides ways to log in and access what an investor needs, but this fails to give that investor the complete picture. You don't have the perspective to get insights into your 401(k) savings in light of your monthly expenditure rate, credit card debt, and rent payments.

This is where the operationally efficient platforms like Mint, by Intuit, step in. If you provide the Mint platform with all of the login and password credentials to your various financial institutions, Mint can bring together a broad, comparative view of your financial situation. This is a significant benefit to the user, similar to what Strava does for your fitness data, and it may well be worth the cost of the platform.

However, there is a cost, and that cost is becoming more and more apparent in recent years. As consumers have allowed (and even begged) for their data to be more accessible so that they could have more operationally efficient lives, they have also handed over the keys to vast amounts of personal data and confidential information. In other words, the cost of having consumer apps and tools that connect all of your relevant financial, health, educational, social, and purchasing data is, in fact, all of your relevant financial, health, educational, social, and purchasing data. Your personal data is the currency with which you purchase this efficiency. And that cost may be too much.

Consider the case of Facebook Connect and Facebook Pixel. The first is the developer capability to log in to a website or app using your Facebook name and password. The second is the advertising pixel (a tiny piece of code on your webpage) that every developer or advertiser that wishes to leverage Facebook ads must deploy onto its site. With millions of sites, apps, and platforms using both of these, people can log in easily and seamlessly across the web or on their phones. They can also like or share any piece of content they find on sites that show the Facebook thumbs-up icons, making their ability to browse and share mindlessly simple.

Unfortunately, and not so obviously, this massively efficient connectivity is also tracking you almost everywhere you go online. Facebook can even trace your offline purchases back to your online, because it knows almost everything you are looking at. By tracking your dwell time on the advertisement for those Cole Haan shoes on Facebook, and then on a site that has the Facebook Pixel, Facebook can coordinate your ID with offline point of sale data to know that you did, in fact, succumb to the desire and buy those great shoes. Add your geolocation data from the Facebook App on your mobile phone pinpointing you in the Cole Haan store, and boom, the circle is complete.

We don't take a position in favor of or against operationally driven data partnerships. All of these examples are mutually beneficial, and provide value to each participant.[29] Data partnership strategies require the honest assessment and understanding of the massively complex interconnectedness of data platforms. Whether your goal is to understand data partnerships as a business or as a consumer, recognize that the operationally efficient data partnership is one of the most important approaches of the last 10 years and will likely continue into the future.

Marketing-Driven Data Partnerships

The marketing-driven data partnership is one in which the alliance of two businesses has a significant marketing benefit to each company. This particular type of relationship is designed to let brands, platforms, or

---

[29] As of writing, several large companies such as Google and Facebook are looking at adding data portability capabilities to their platforms (see Kevin McLaughlin, "Tech Giants Letting Users Move Data Between Web Services," The Information, August 2018, www.theinformation.com/briefings/30b414).

datasets get value from each other in an open, aggressive marketing strategy designed to benefit both companies.

The most obvious version of this partnership type is the app marketplace. Popularized in the consumer space by Apple's App Store and the Google Play Store, these markets have grown to millions of applications available from third-party platforms, integrated directly into the experience of Apple and Google products. These integrations have led to incredible success stories for some small, innovative companies, but they have equally benefited massive corporations looking to ensure that their customers can access innovative tools anywhere.

The marketing advantage, however, is another true benefit to these partnerships. These platforms' contracts include clauses limiting the use of each company's trademarks, logos, and brand guides. These are carefully written because these large platforms know that companies building an app for a particular ecosystem want to get benefits from the brand identity and value of their app marketplace provider.

Realistically, apps with runaway success — like Pokémon GO, Angry Birds, or even Urbanspoon — are very rare. Most app development today revolves around the potential of an opportunity — including, of course, the opportunity to add Google and Apple icons to the app developers' marketing, offering strength by association. And let us not forget that Google, Apple, and other app markets benefit from every single app added to their market. The competition to have the largest app store is fierce, and these platforms benefit from receiving a portion of the revenue every app generates. The marketing benefit to both parties is obvious.

App markets will continue to evolve, and you should constantly evaluate current and new markets for integration opportunities. Salesforce's AppExchange, ServiceNow, Infusionsoft, and Marketo: the list of potential platforms to integrate with is as varied as the apps themselves, and you must review each for its value and marketing benefit. While you can elect to wait for a customer to ask for you to create the integration, marketing-driven data partnerships offer additional benefits.

First, the opportunity to access co-marketing dollars is a critical contractual and negotiation point. Co-marketing is an increasingly popular relationship in which two companies agree to jointly commit resources, content, promotions, or events to a partnership. Because an integration typically requires effort on the part of both parties, the desire to get a return for the effort is substantial. Further, the marketing departments of many companies are looking for new ways to highlight their approach to data usage to position themselves as innovative. Co-marketing can take many forms, but the goal from a partnership perspective is to quickly identify the value proposition of the integration and to then carve out messaging that benefits each platform.

While advertising budgets are the most obvious co-marketing approach, budgetary constraints need not get in the way of designing a proactive co-marketing campaign. Webinars, seminars, blog posts, training, and field events offer outstanding benefits and typically cost very little to build out and promote. Field events can be expensive, but rather than create new field marketing events, leverage current events to get both platforms onstage or in some sort of pre-existing agenda to highlight the new data partnership and the many benefits it may bring mutual customers and prospects.

Summarizing the Mutually Beneficial Data Partnership

You should find partnerships that are mutually beneficial to your company, your data, and your clients. These partnerships are driven by customers, operational efficiency, or by shared marketing opportunities. Form a team within your company that specifically identifies these types of partnership opportunities, with someone from your executive team as the sponsor. Encourage employees to make suggestions and to poll customers regularly for ways that your company could engage with other platforms the customer uses. Celebrate mutually beneficial partnerships internally and externally, and you will attract additional players to the table.

11

Channel Data Partnerships

CHANNEL DATA PARTNERSHIPS HAVE been around in the financial services and the marketing industry for decades. Every Bloomberg terminal or Thomson Reuters platform is a descendent of a long line of data systems designed to gather market and financial data and deliver it through a channel platform and reseller arrangement. The concept of selling data in large quantities or for specific purposes continues to evolve rapidly. And because any transmission of significant amounts of data triggers security and oversight concerns, these types of partnerships are challenging from a compliance perspective as well.

Channel data partnerships enable data distribution across distributed platforms, distributed sales teams, or both. While every data broker or reseller has unique contracts and partnership agreements, we've created an overview of their most common and important elements. Because channel data partnerships include both data partnerships and revenue generation, we describe both aspects. We will also help you protect your data assets and your company reputation in such partnerships.

The Two Flavors of Channel Data Partnerships

Channel data partnerships fall typically into two primary categories: affiliate programs and reseller programs. Both involve channel data partners, which we define as companies that represent or resell data from suppliers.

In the simplest of terms, an affiliate program is one in which the channel data partner acts as an affiliate, introducing potential customers to your data and information and receiving a percentage of the fee you ultimately charge those customers. The affiliate should be qualified to explain the basics of your data and the value it may have for a particular prospect. Once the affiliate makes the introduction, you are typically responsible for closing the sale and managing the customer relationship. When your sales process is complex, or the use of your data requires significant expertise, the affiliate usually doesn't add much value. Also, because affiliate sellers represent multiple suppliers, they only know the basics about each dataset they represent.

The second approach to channel data partnerships is the reseller program. In reseller partnerships, the data supplier sells the dataset to the reseller partner at a wholesale rate, and the reseller partner is then free to mark up and sell the data at the price it determines. The reseller closes each sale and manages the ongoing customer relationship. This arrangement allows a data provider to focus on its data business and turn customer relationships and management over to the reseller. In this case, you must put significant effort into training and preparing the reseller to understand the data and to be proficient in all aspects of its use. Reseller partnerships work well for easily understood datasets but can generate channel conflicts.

Affiliate Channel Data Partnerships

Data platforms, markets, and brokers use affiliate programs to identify new datasets, quickly test their market demand, and rapidly exploit the opportunity. Affiliate teams focus on finding the next great dataset and introducing it to their clients first, with the hope of grabbing the agreed-upon commission. Commissions to an affiliate range from 5 percent to 50 percent, depending on exclusivity, appeal, and the proven track record of the affiliate's team of sellers in market.

As the data supplier in the affiliate channel partnership, you choose the price and manner in which your data is sold. Affiliate deals include guides on prices that the affiliate seller is permitted to share with prospects, but in contrast to reseller agreements, you have the final call on pricing. The best affiliate partners helpfully provide market demand feedback on your "ballpark" pricing. Don't rely too heavily on this feedback, however, because affiliate sellers can sometimes seek to lower prices to speed up deals and improve their own top-line revenue.

One real benefit of an affiliate introducing your data product is that you are still in control of the customer relationship post-sale. In other words, your team gets to work directly with each new customer to promote the customer's successful use of the data. While this requires resources on your part, it enables you to suggest additional data, services, and guidance to those customers. The "land and expand" model, in which you sell through an affiliate in one geography or with one derivative dataset, naturally opens the door to expanded revenue potential. Negotiate carefully regarding the scope of products, services, and datasets for which you must pay a commission to an affiliate. A fair approach is to specify which solutions were directly attributable to the effort of the affiliate seller, but to exclude commissions on upsells into additional services.

Affiliate data partnership contracts need to clearly outline the terms of commission eligibility. Initially, many affiliate sales organizations push for a perpetual payment for as long as the customer continues to pay for the data. This is an unrealistic burden on the data provider. You should negotiate a declining commission schedule for a maximum of two years, after which you owe no further commission to the affiliate. Sending a significant commission payment to an introducing agent who has not added further value to the customer relationship is an unsustainable drag on your revenue growth. You will need those dollars to reward your own customer success team for the hard work they are doing to retain and grow the customer.

Some Warnings with Affiliate Channel Data Partnerships

Having worked for and with hundreds of data platforms and data brokers over the years, we've identified the most common pitfalls with the affiliate model. Design your contracts to avoid these issues.

Overrepresentation
We have worked with data marts and data brokers that represent thousands of data providers in an affiliate model. This overrepresentation creates a

host of problems. First, affiliate sellers cannot possibly know each product or dataset well enough to add consistent value as they introduce it. No matter how the affiliate works to understand the benefits of your data, it represents too many partners to understand the comprehensive features of each. Sellers tend to focus on the "flavor of the month" or freshest dataset because they have only so much bandwidth.

You may not be able to overcome this issue because some of the bigger data platforms and brokers are necessary partners, depending on your dataset and the industry you are targeting. Instead, focus on finding out the pricing and terms with which affiliates are engaging with datasets similar to yours. Often, they don't mind sharing their financial and commission terms for other data providers, so you can work to partner on slightly better terms than your competition to stand out from the crowd. You need to incent the affiliate sales team over your competition.

In the previous chapter, we discussed co-marketing to create a mutually beneficial relationship. When a potential affiliate partner represents too large a number of other datasets, add a co-marketing clause in your contract to focus it more on your data. If the affiliate has sufficient market reach and a strong reputation, negotiate joint press releases, webinars, and training materials to ensure that the affiliate focuses on your data.

Misrepresentation of Data
Any time you allow another company or business to represent your data, its quality, or its value, you run the risk of misrepresentation or exaggeration.

Contractually specify training and ongoing assessment of your affiliate's reseller staff. A simple certification guide and exam can be an excellent way to ensure that sellers don't overpromise or misguide customers. Because you ultimately are involved in the pricing and final sale of the data in the affiliate relationship, you should also institute a clear, ongoing protocol for revisiting and re-explaining the value proposition of the data you have, and how it can or cannot be utilized. Some successful partnerships we have seen employ a secondary, follow-up phone call, prior to an account being marked as closed or invoiced, in which your customer support and account management team will walk the customer through the exact value proposition one last time. Because your client success or account management team is paid to retain and improve a customer's experience (and not on the sales price of the initial transaction), people on the team are astute at identifying potential misalignments of the data value. While it can be uncomfortable to turn away an otherwise completed sale, it is far better than having a new customer with unrealistic expectations.

Overpromise, Under-deliver in Sales

One common issue in affiliate relationships is the affiliate's promise to deliver sales. If you truly want a promise of sales, then make a reseller agreement; affiliate programs typically don't guarantee sales or revenue.

Affiliate seller programs often represent their number of selling staff, reach across an industry, and overall reach as they introduce your data. Unfortunately, you need to evaluate those numbers in context based on the number of other datasets they are selling, or that they *have ever sold*. Because every customer maintains only so much bandwidth for dealing or exploring new datasets, an overactive affiliate program can quickly burn up all available customer cycles and end up not doing justice to any dataset.

The best way to avoid this problem is to negotiate an early termination clause and then identify selling problems early. No affiliate platform should be surprised when you ask for this type of "out" in your agreement. Naturally, to be fair to the affiliate, if it has been successful in selling even one relationship with your team, you should be prepared to offer a wind-down that continues to pay its commission. Our preferred wind-down period is one year, but two years is not unheard of.

Affiliate Channel Conflict

While channel conflict is much more common with resellers, there can still be conflict between your direct sales program and your affiliate sellers. The typical problem occurs when an affiliate program salesperson calls upon a prospect that is already in the pipeline of one of your own sales employees, or vice versa. You can build ways to resolve this into your contracts upfront.

The single best method to deal with channel conflict is to track every lead, prospect, customer, and status thoroughly. Insist that your affiliate partners provide you with an ongoing list of current prospects they are working with or pitching your data to, which will allow you track these leads and manage your internal team appropriately. Then incorporate, where appropriate, a time window associated with any introduction. Depending upon the complexity of your data or the price of your solution, introductions may need months to close. You can typically justify a six-month window or similar timeframe where a current prospect moves from being associated with the affiliate seller to being, once again, an available prospect for your sales team.

When a dispute does arise between an affiliate channel data partnership and your own team, work diligently to maintain trust on both sides of the agreement. A strong affiliate relationship is important to maintain, but so is the faith your internal sellers feel toward their right to earn a living. The best course of action is to define a split-commission structure when you can't agree upon a clear owner of the lead or prospect. This way, both teams will gain some of the sales commission, and you should be able to prevent channel conflict from breaking down the trust between your organization and the affiliate sales organization. While this may lead to sometimes paying duplicate sales commissions, the goodwill maintained can be well worth the additional expense.

Reseller Channel Data Partnerships

Every time you boot up Netflix or Hulu or even your cable television box, if you still have that sort of thing, you are witnessing a reseller channel data partnership. In each of these cases, the content that comes as part of the base subscription has been purchased through a reseller contract where the provider or producer of the data (or media in this case) has been paid in full and the platform, like Netflix, can now choose how or what to charge for access to that data and content. Amazon Prime Video, however, is a hybrid model, where some content has been purchased through a reseller agreement (these videos have a "Prime" ribbon on the top left corner of their cover art image), and where other content must be purchased for an additional cost. The content included with your Amazon Prime subscription is an example of a reseller channel data partnership while the content that requires an additional purchase is an example of the affiliate data partnerships we described in the previous section.

Data providers get many advantages from working with resellers — most notably, scale and distribution. If your company needs distribution and scale, perhaps in a particular new market or geography, don't miss the opportunity to have an established provider of similar data solutions represent your content and deliver it. They can open an entire market quickly.

When you work through a reseller, you typically don't maintain a relationship with the end customer who is utilizing your data. The reseller has the direct contract with the customer and is responsible for the entire sale as well as the post-sale activity with the customer. This is both a blessing and a curse, depending upon your vision for your data business. By relinquishing the control over the customer relationship, you are granting significant leverage to your resellers because they may eventually use that control in negotiating price or terms with you. On the other hand, if you are a smaller operation or one that is content to operate in a different market from the ones where you employ a reseller, you don't need to employ nearly as large a team to service customers because that burden has been shifted to your reseller partner.

Pricing is an important characteristic of reseller channel data partnerships. Often, reseller terms are vastly more complex than affiliate deals, where one or two commission rates suffice. Resellers expect sliding wholesale discounts that are directly tied to the volume of purchases, so you need to develop different pricing tiers. The key here is to focus upon the commitment level of the reseller. In other words, you should never just adjust pricing as a reseller sells more licenses of your data. Instead, you should negotiate upfront that the reseller will commit to a specific tier in order to gain more favorable pricing. In this way, your data company can forecast and expect revenue from the reseller upfront rather than calculate its wholesale rate after the applicable time period has closed. By focusing on commitment-level pricing strategies, you are properly aligning your reseller partner's focus on sales, training, marketing, and servicing with your own goals. Reseller arrangements that don't include significant monetary commitments are nothing more than affiliate agreements in sheep's clothing.

Summarizing: reseller arrangements provide rapid scale, committed revenue, and operational savings because you don't have to necessarily support each end customer.

Some Warnings with Reseller Channel Data Partnerships

Reseller relationships have several unsuspected drawbacks. Resellers control the customer relationship and therefore the ongoing value proposition. This lack of direct client relationship can have significant business ramifications as you grow and expand your data offering.

Channel Conflict with Direct Sellers
One of the best reasons to engage with a reseller is to scale your sales operations quickly. Unfortunately, because you are empowering the reseller's own sales team, you are also creating a competitive force to your own direct sellers. For this reason, many smaller data companies' sales teams focus only on identifying new reseller or affiliate partnerships, and effectively stay out of direct competition with their reseller partners.

If you do choose to have a direct sales team calling on the same or similar customers to those that your resellers will call upon, you need proactive solutions to keep everyone focused on selling to the appropriate customer set. You can segment the market and potential customer base into different targets. This allows your internal sales team to focus on a patch of prospects that differ from the resellers'. We have seen internal sales teams behave incredibly badly toward resellers. To avoid this, involve your sales leadership in reseller contracts and get their approval and support early on.

As a data company grows, it eventually will move into direct sales and will compete with its reseller partners. If this is your intent, it is better to plan ahead for how you will eventually wind down the partnerships without harming the end customer relationship. We have seen countless examples of poorly managed breakups between resellers and their data suppliers that naturally bleed over to the end customer having a bad experience.

Misrepresentation of Data or Capabilities
Misrepresentation problems play out differently in reseller agreements. A typical reseller arrangement will allow for a reseller to integrate your data directly into their offering in constructive ways. This can be an excellent opportunity to showcase the data and its capabilities, but it can also lead to misunderstandings. We'll demonstrate the risks with an illustrative example of misrepresentation in one context: user reviews.

The manner and proximity with which your data is represented within a reseller's platform can confuse the value proposition and even the definition of the data. In earlier chapters, we discussed how various datasets can be analyzed together based upon common factors such as time or place. The problem is that many times, a reseller may attempt to force different datasets together to help strengthen their story. For example, some digital marketing companies form partnerships to access reviews about a particular business or place. When they do this, they typically show the reviews for a business from several different review platforms and sources. Unfortunately, reviews come in many different styles and don't all apply equally to a business. In one case, we witnessed product reviews merged with business reviews merged with personnel reviews; the resulting combined pages were quite confused. There are times when mashing different datasets together is helpful, but sometimes it can just cause confusion. Just because a massive Toyota auto dealership has a five-year-old used Audi on their lot for sale does not mean that every review of every Audi model is appropriate to be included on their website.

For data partnerships and reseller arrangements this confusion can come back to harm your brand, particularly if other sources that your data is adjacent to do not share your adherence to quality. Yelp, for example, has worked tirelessly for years to maintain top quality in the much-maligned business reviews space. Yelp employs very strict guidelines for partnerships and, while it will allow some of its data to be made available by resellers of its services, it always seeks to ensure that its data is not commingled or lost in a sea of other reviews providers of questionable quality and authenticity. Many resellers, while understanding the concern, still want to push all reviews data into one unified interface, which can lead to a misunderstanding of the data. If Yelp, within its own data, rates a business as only three stars, while three other sources of reviews rate the business as a perfect five stars (perhaps through some unfair manipulation by the business owner), then merging all of those ratings into a four-star experience (or higher) is not really demonstrating the value, quality, or authenticity of Yelp data.

One last warning: we have seen several resellers merge data sets from multiple sources to desensitizing end customers to the source quality of their partner's data. Once they've removed that sensitivity, they can eventually delete a high-quality source and replace it with cheaper, lesser quality sources, improving the reseller's margins. With regard to reviews, some platforms have merged review sources to slowly replace higher quality sources of data with lower quality ones. Unfortunately, the end customer will slowly lose a grasp on the value of the data as all restaurants are averaged across data sources to a score of, roughly, 4.2 stars. Then, at the right time, the reseller can remove the most expensive or restrictive data partnerships. Be on guard for these partnership pitfalls and monitor closely how channel resellers integrate, manage, display, and identify your data along with similar datasets.

Pricing Power Erosion
The initial revenue guaranteed by large resellers is invigorating. The larger the commitment from the reseller, the larger the discount it expects for your data services. Because committed revenue is so critical to growth, the trade-off seems worthwhile, until the reseller begins to offer your data service priced at a fraction of what other resellers charge or what your own team can offer directly.

Optimally, your contracts with resellers need to address price ranges or acceptable bands of pricing. Your legal team will need to determine how and when these bands are appropriate, and they must draft them in compliance with local laws. While some jurisdictions do not allow tightly controlled price setting in reseller contracts, there are other ways to ensure that partners adhere to a certain expected level of pricing in their outward-facing customer contracts. If all else fails, a right to terminate for any reason with proper notice may be the only way to ensure that you can quickly shut down a reseller that is disrupting your pricing in a market.

Another pricing issue with resellers is confidentiality. Resellers can be a little too open with each other about their contracts with data providers. When pricing information, which is normally confidential, leaks to the market, this creates pricing pressure on data providers. Salespeople and operational employees move from reseller to reseller, bringing with them the knowledge of what a data provider's deal was at their previous employer. This erosion of pricing power can very quickly create headwinds in your pricing strategy. Industry conferences are particularly dangerous, as commoditized competitors to your dataset will race to spread pricing information they uncover about your data from other resellers or partners.

One way to handle these "loose lips" issues is to devise a consistent and fair approach to pricing from the beginning. If you are going to provide discounts for upfront commitments by reseller partnerships, the scale should be consistent and set in stone. This gives your company defensible practices that work in your favor. Additionally, you can elect to segment or provide different datasets to different reseller partners. In this way, each price paid by a reseller reflects not only the commitment level of the reseller but also a particular basket, timeline, or segment of data.

Concentration of Revenue
Reseller channel data partnerships can quickly come to represent substantial portions of your overall data revenue. Because the commitments for thousands of users are guaranteed upfront or over some specified ramp-up period, this revenue can be critical for growth and stability. Unfortunately, it can also present the "too many eggs in one basket" problem, in which a few resellers represent more than 10 percent of a data provider's overall revenue.

A reseller that understands the leverage they have over your data revenue can be dangerous because the reseller gains significant pricing advantage. Just as with any concentration-of-revenue problem, there will be features, terms, pricing, and replacement issues with these resellers, rapidly turning them from friend to rival. If a reseller represents a significant share of your revenue, you also need to prepare for a price war with other data providers that want to replace you at the reseller. In the end, each party, including the reseller partner, will do what is best for its own business. This could mean negotiating a lower price with you or cancelling the contract with you altogether, electing instead to partner with your competitor.

Manage this risk through better data products and reseller diversification. By constantly improving and expanding your data offering, you can maintain pricing authority over your competition. Engaging with many resellers and partners will help diversify the customer base and limit the power that any individual reseller has over your company. In both cases, speed of improvement is the key. Product and data innovation must be just as fast as your teams' ability to sign new resellers and get them to market.

One final issue to consider with revenue concentration: when a data product or solution becomes aligned with one or only a few resellers in a given market, other resellers may choose to specifically avoid your dataset so they can claim to have a "unique" offering differentiated from their competitors. If your dataset has competitors or lacks differentiation, a large reseller relationship can create an unspoken bias against your dataset.

Channel Data Partnership Hybrid Models

As we have discussed, the two models of affiliate or reseller channel data partnerships cover the majority of scenarios you will encounter as you bring your dataset to market. There are also hybrid opportunities. Hybrids attempt to mitigate some of the risks noted above by segmenting the opportunities or sales territories for each program.

For example, when you have a direct sales team and wish to employ a channel data partnership approach as well, sales conflicts are bound to occur where one team feels the other is blocking them or, worse, has stolen a commission or opportunity. To prevent this, create a hybrid model that separates commissions based upon the size of the customer being sold to. In this way, your company can have partners that sell to small businesses as a reseller but may only sell to larger businesses as an affiliate. This approach has the additional benefit of ensuring that your partner handles smaller customers' service while your team handles larger customers' service. Because you own the direct client relationship in affiliate transactions, this aligns your internal team to make the most of each introduction to the largest customers.

Because your direct sales team is the most experienced and knowledgeable about the dataset they represent full-time, they should be focused on bringing in the largest deals. Resellers and affiliates, on the other hand, are better at representing several different solutions and may have a host of different datasets in their offering from different providers. Allowing your channel data partners to resell your data to smaller businesses is a great way to scale your business as you limit partners only to sales that aren't huge opportunities for your internal sales team. Marking a limit to the opportunity size — perhaps by factors like target company revenue, employee count, licenses needed, or any other reasonably appropriate metric that draws the line for a prospective customer size — will keep the reseller from battling your direct sales team.

If you employ this strategy, it will be a sensitive subject with your resellers. Reseller partners typically want to also sell to large businesses, and they don't love the concept of being limited to just smaller client opportunities. This is why it is your responsibility to make the affiliate solution, where the partner receives compensation for large-opportunity introductions, part of a compelling compromise. Whether financially through a large percentage revenue share, or through a type of exclusivity, or other favorable terms, it is vital that you maintain a positive relationship where you reward introductions by channel data partners to help your team on both the low and high ends of the market.

Hybrid models deliver both the reseller scale and the affiliate control of the customer that data providers desire. The negotiation on such models can be difficult to complete, but if all parties are honest about their actual capabilities, you can identify the right mixture of models together. Unfortunately, we have seen many partnerships fail at the goal line because of the less-than-humble attitude by one side or both as to their own team's sales and service capabilities. As we pointed out in the introduction to this book, partnerships require two keys to success: leadership and humility. In channel data partnerships, the latter is often very difficult to maintain during each negotiation.

Segmentation Strategies

One of the best ways to build out your channel data partnership strategy is to identify a segmentation strategy for your products and services. By segmenting your solution, you can keep resellers, affiliates, and direct sales teams from running headfirst into each other in the market. The benefits can protect both you and your channel data partnerships, but can make tracking complex. There are countless ways to segment a data offering, but most are combinations of four approaches.

Data or Product Segmentation

We have analyzed many strategies that segment a data offering. You can use depth, timeliness, or coverage to segment data. In each case, you offer a particular *combination* of datasets to each partner or group of partners focused on a particular client base. For example, you can segment your offering by providing the data over a historical timeframe as one product, versus a real-time delivery approach for another. Perhaps only affiliates could introduce the real-time solution, while resellers could show historical data after a certain time embargo. This is how many data providers segment stock charts and price data as well as other fundamental financial datasets.

You can successfully segment data by depth, with certain details or fields being reserved to only certain partnerships. For example, some business valuation data may only be available at a sector or market level through one partner while the individual company valuation analysis is reserved for bigger partners with larger commitments to the product.

Lastly, you can use derivative datasets to create segmentation. When your channel data partner has its own unique data, an ideal strategy is to merge your data with your partner's to create a derivative work, only available through the partner. Consider the Zillow Zestimate, which makes an estimation of any home price by merging, analyzing, and calculating values based on dozens of different data sources. If you were one of the data partners that provide data to Zillow, you could eliminate competition with your other partners by limiting Zillow's use of your data to their Zestimate calculation. In this way, your particular dataset may not be fully revealed but only exist as a component of the Zestimate, thus ensuring this partnership doesn't adversely affect other opportunities for your data products.

Geographic Segmentation

Data knows no borders, and yet geography is still a very popular way to segment your data partnership strategy. We have seen many successful partnerships segmented by country or even continent. We do not recommend segmenting into any smaller geographic regions than at the country level.

To segment by country, start by identifying the market dynamics at work. Is the country more monopolistic in the way businesses operate, or does it tend to be more fragmented and competitive for data, like yours? How does this vary by industry? Empower one partner in a monopolistic environment but use a more diversified strategy in openly competitive markets. One common approach is to segment data that is geographically about a particular region to partners in that region. By combining these two segmentation strategies, you can ensure that your chosen partnerships are protected from interference from other resellers.

Sectors and Industry Segmentations
Depending upon the depth and breadth of your data assets in each area, segmenting your data solutions by sector and industry can be a smart approach. We recently worked with a company that could successfully mine, analyze, and continually improve data about local businesses. Upon going to market, this company recognized that the legal industry and medical professions had very specific data needs that easily allowed for segmentation. In this way, they were able to secure separate channel data partnerships with a firm that specialized in marketing solutions to only the legal industry and another targeting the medical industry. Segmenting along these lines meant that their own internal sales team was given free rein over all other verticals while the two channel data partnerships could keep control over their respective markets.

Client Size and Opportunity Size
The last approach to data segmentation is to review the size of the prospective customer, or the overall opportunity size of the customer. If a potential customer is global in size or massive in their overall revenue opportunity, you may need a dedicated seller from your own firm to maximize that sale and deliver the appropriate service level. Smaller companies seeking to buy your data, on the other hand, may require or expect less assistance.

When building your channel data partnership strategy, regardless of affiliate, reseller, or hybrid approaches, you should review your current client base and identify any likely segments that can be built into your contracts with partners. Sometimes the segments are obvious based on your prior successes and failures to market your data directly. Choose a sizing segmentation metric that is easy to understand and fair to all parties involved.

Summarizing Channel Data Partnerships

When applied properly, a channel data partnership strategy can greatly increase the sales and service scale of your data business. The benefits are too great to ignore, and for many companies seeking to build a data business, these are some of the best approaches to take to open up new markets where they historically have had little to no involvement. Finding new customers, legitimizing your data offering, and scaling up quickly are just a few of the reasons you should seriously consider building out a channel approach.

Review the differences between the affiliate and reseller approaches and whether or not a hybrid model is optimal. While it can be difficult to choose the right strategy at the outset, changing it after launching can generate major problems. When building your strategy, it is important that you commit to it for at least a couple of years, because your data partners will demand some level of stability. No one likes joining a game where the rules of engagement change too frequently, and channel data partnerships are no different.

Part IV: Protect

12

Protecting Data and Reputations

THE FINAL STEP IN the DataSmart Method is *Protect*. While it's the last step, it's certainly not the least important. Protecting your data assets is a never-ending pursuit and should be part of every discussion and decision you make regarding data. As we explain how to adopt this mentality, remember that each step of the DataSmart Method offers the opportunity for protective thinking. Don't wait until the end to think this way; analyze your risks throughout your planning and execution, as we describe in this chapter.

Let's start by reviewing how you need to protect your data assets at each step in the DataSmart Method.

Step 1: Identify

In part I, we focused on identifying all of your company's intrinsic and extrinsic data assets. We described how this demands a change in mindset, expanding your attention beyond the typical day-to-day operations to the additional data you create. Sometimes this change in focus can also reveal areas of your business where your company is not protecting data properly.

As you go through the identification process, take stock of the data itself, as well as where it is stored, who has access, and what protections are built into your current systems. Here's a case in point: Just recently, we went to an auto dealer to test drive a new vehicle. The salesperson asked if they could make a quick photocopy of a driver's license before handing over the keys. This is standard practice in auto dealerships and seems reasonable, as they are literally allowing you to drive off in one of their vehicles. But this seemingly simple and routine exchange of data got us thinking about where auto dealers keep these copies of licenses and how they protect them. If this auto dealer had followed the *Identify* process, it would have quickly inventoried this stack of driver's license photocopies as a historical record of every test drive and as a potential customer lead list. At the same time, this collection of copies of private citizens' government IDs should also set off alarm bells around privacy, access, and security. In the same way, you should use the *Identify* step to inventory not only all of your data assets but also the potential data protection issues that surround each.

Step 2: Value

In the *Value* process, you set the range of values for each dataset. You must do this not only from your own business perspective, but also from the perspective of the original provider of the data — for example, your customer. Valuation of data assets is a balance between the monetizable worth in the data that partners or customers are willing to pay and the risks of keeping, maintaining, and processing that data. You must carefully weigh the value of a data element against the risk of maintaining it. As data privacy laws gain traction throughout the world, more and more countries will demand a humanized approach toward data, and each business must balance this with the actual business value that any individual dataset can produce.

Prioritizing datasets from a valuation perspective helps you to align your protective approach to those values for each of your datasets. We don't keep the milk in a safe and neither should you. Focus on the most valuable datasets you have from both your and the original data owners' perspectives and then analyze carefully how you are managing their protection. This is also a great time to focus on your compliance with data protection laws, which may have specific requirements regarding how you are permitted to handle certain datasets. One goal of the *Value* step of the DataSmart Method is to decide whether or not you really need a certain piece of data. Just as you should assess whether you need or will ever use that treadmill currently serving as a coat rack in the basement, you should critically assess the value of your data.

Step 3: Structure

As you build your data partnership strategies, you need proper legal and technical protections. As we've described in part III, when you enter the *Structure* phase with potential partners, you must follow some very detailed steps. You must also consider these questions: Who are you about to partner with? Did you review their reputation, and their current partners, clients, and affiliations? Do you know any of their current partners that you could reach out to for references? Do their website or materials discuss data security and privacy? Have they appointed a DPO?

Many great companies are being dragged through the mud lately because they agreed to partner with companies that misuse data. The heaping mess that is the Facebook and Cambridge Analytica case clearly qualifies. Could it have been avoided? When Cambridge Analytica and Aleksandr Kogan collaborated to obtain Facebook user data through an app, they clearly deviated from the confines of Facebook's partner review process. But the ease with which this sidestepping took place demonstrates that Facebook did not adequately recognize the reputational risk associated with data integration by its partners. Even while pundits rush to hate on Facebook, the reality is that much of the data that Cambridge Analytica was accessing has always been a part of Facebook integrations and this wasn't abnormal in terms of a data relationship. It was how Cambridge Analytica gathered and used the data it obtained through the partnership that threw this dataset into a whole new light. Facebook failed in its responsibility to continuously review data partner sharing or institute the kind of controls that would have prevented misuse on this scale. The lesson is clear, though: when structuring data partnerships, it is your responsibility to build a protective approach legally, technically, and operationally to ensure ongoing compliance.

Step 4: Protect

With the prior steps now as backdrop, you can see that in each phase of the DataSmart Method, there are opportunities to align your goals with a protective focus. By constantly challenging your approach, you will improve your chances to identify issues early that might cost you dearly, and then structure deals to mitigate risk. Let's now turn our attention to more protections you should consider for your organization.

Data Protection Officer

Based on our experience in our law firm, you should be considering a data protection officer. As the name suggests, this is an officer-level position dedicated to the protection of your data. People typically confuse this role with the roles of the chief information officer, chief data officer, or chief technology officer. Each position's responsibilities are actually different, although one of those individuals could technically fulfill the role of DPO. If data protection is a clear part of their job this may make sense. The real difference though, is that none of those other C-level roles is mandated by Europe's General Data Protection Regulation. The GDPR applies to companies that market or sell to Europe, even if the company isn't itself located in the European Union. And even if your company does not have a presence in Europe, the concept of appointing a competent, capable individual to oversee your data security and privacy policies is simple good sense, regardless of whether it is a legal requirement, for reasons we set forth below.

The DPO is responsible for the ongoing protection of customer data and sensitive data within an organization. They represent the customers' interest in protecting data at the company they work for, and the company's own interest in complying with data security laws. Additionally, companies that are mandated to have a DPO under the terms of the GDPR cannot terminate the DPO simply for doing their job. The DPO is protected, and therefore has the ability to give unbiased counsel and guidance. This is a unique situation that helps ensure that companies required to appoint a DPO are also not permitted to prevent the DPO from representing the best interest of their customers (or data subjects).

A DPO is supposed to speak up for the data, and the individuals that the data represents. In chapter 2 we explained that most data of business value is actually about a person. That understanding is crucial to the faithful execution of the role of the DPO. The GDPR mandates a DPO for those businesses that process large amounts of personal data or engage in ongoing tracking and monitoring of personal data. Consult your regulatory experts to determine if a DPO is mandatory for your business. Even if it isn't, we believe most companies should have one.

The DPO works alongside of the other C-suite officers at your firm and maintains Data Protection Authority rules and regulations. This means that they should be expert or well-versed in the GDPR and all of its requirements, but it also means that the DPO needs to understand other jurisdictional requirements around the world in places your business operates. This responsibility is a serious one, and you should review the information available at the International Association of Privacy Professionals (IAPP) for further clarity.[30] The IAPP is the world's largest information privacy community and provides comprehensive data privacy and regulatory certification training.

Because you have gotten this far, you must believe that your business has opportunities to create value through your data and data partnerships. You have also certainly noticed the seemingly daily disastrous headlines about data breaches plaguing companies. There have been hundreds of different data breaches involving more than 30,000 records each; some of these breaches affected hundreds of millions of data subjects. There may be others we don't know of yet, as well as additional breaches that affected fewer records. The actual instances of data being misused, stolen, or mishandled are too numerous to track.

When gurus say that "data is the new currency,"[31] they typically are discussing ways you can transact and make money with your data. But data is subject to the same risks as currency, including theft, embezzlement, counterfeiting, and seizure. Once you understand data as currency, you recognize why you must put forth the same effort toward protecting data as you do to protecting financial accounts and access to your business coffers. This is why we consider the DPO to be just as essential as the CFO.

The DPO is authorized to work throughout a business to review any practices related to the data of the business and its customers. This implies a close working relationship with every division and manager, but also a comprehensive, firm-wide view of data assets. Don't overlook the need for

---

30   See https://iapp.org.
31   We said this in the first paragraph of this book, so...

strong interpersonal and communications skills for your DPO. While they aren't responsible for creating data partnerships, the DPO is the ideal person to review each arrangement for potential risks or threats. Your finance department includes roles to help you identify risky behavior; you could similarly use a sheriff for data protection practices across your company.

Data Audit Teams

It fascinates us how few data audit teams we run into, regardless of company size or data asset library depth. Everyone is accustomed to financial audits; the very same principles can be put to work for your data strategy to monitor intrinsic and extrinsic data usage. Data audit teams systematically review and document the usage, access, and financial linkage of data throughout an organization. They are a hybrid between bean counters and data geeks.

Create this team, or hire a data audit lead to create it, and you will immediately increase data protection focus around the organization. Typically, a data audit team will begin with a review of systems and access logs to identify who is using what. You will be shocked at how much data is accessible by people within your organization that should not have access to it. If you don't already have a team reviewing all of your log files to track users and access points, then your data audit team will start with that. This is also the first moment where your new data audit team will make some enemies. Usually some manager "who has always had access before" will be upset that the audit turned up their access and usage. Be prepared for this type of response: it's a sign that you've caught something problematic.

Once the data audit team has used log files to document and then restrict access to data, it continues with an interview process within each division. The goal of internal interviews is to work with the rank-and-file employees to find out what they use data for, whether their use and access is necessary, and how you can better protect the information. Many companies restrict their audit interviews to managers, but this can be counterproductive. When you consider that every newsletter signup, Twitter account, purchase, customer service complaint, and website hit affects several different employees at your company, you realize that those are the people closest to the data and they often have the best understanding of how it is (or is not) used.

Interviews reveal the social hierarchy of data access at your business. There are engineers that have access to every transaction at your company, although they aren't in sales or accounting. They can see all the transactions, including the financial terms, because they built the database in which this data often resides. Even if it is encrypted in storage, these employees typically have also built (and have the keys for) the encryption module. This isn't necessarily a problem, but it illustrates the types of insight you might get from interviewing an employee who is boastful about their access, or from another employee lamenting their lack thereof.

Once the access logs and interviews are all buttoned up, the data audit team will flip around their green visors and determine the financial metrics. This is our favorite part of the process because it so closely aligns with step two of the DataSmart Method, *Value*. The data audit team will connect access and loss or misappropriation of data to potential financial impacts. For example, one company we worked with had hundreds of salespeople who could provide "free trial" access to a dataset for a period of 30 days. For some datasets, this generates a lead, helps demonstrate value, and engages prospective customers. The data audit team at this company discovered that there was no process tracking the number of times a customer received a free trial or how many times the free-trial period was extended for an additional 30 days. They tabulated thousands of these additional "months" of access over a period of only one year. At a cost of around $500 per month, these accounts misused data with a value of more than $1 million in one year. Data teams always pay for themselves by revealing such activities.

This was more an example of poor sales training than malfeasance. Many times, the data audit team will help with issues in identifying and valuing data, which then leads to better data governance. However, the data audit team also improves the overall corporate culture and attitude toward data security in general. From the day you announce the arrival of a data audit team empowered to review access and usage of all company data assets, you will see employees and practices change. Rats will jump ship and reckless drivers will suddenly position their hands at ten and two.

Data Security and Technology Safeguards

Data security is no mystery: typing the phrase "data security" into Amazon will return over 3,000 books dedicated to the topic. We're not here to tell you how to do security; instead, we want to outline the security elements you should pay attention to when building data partnerships.

First, data partnerships must include security-specific provisions. With financial institutions and healthcare-focused businesses, these provisions make an entire separate document, usually referred to as the data security questionnaire or addendum. These documents are becoming more standard across different verticals, and we recommend that you ask about them in your opening meetings with a potential partner. We say this because there likely will be certain practices, protocols, and programs required by your potential data partner that you don't currently employ. When your CTO, CIO, and DPO review the questionnaire and addendum, you don't want there to be a sudden surprise challenge that your team says is insurmountable. By enlisting the input and help of your technology team as early as possible in a data partnership discussion that requires specific security documentation, you will give your team the best chance at success. You also will likely maintain a healthier relationship with your technology leadership; avoid the common mistake of inviting these individuals late to the party.

Second, data security in a legal document between two parties becomes obsolete rapidly. The contract and due diligence required to get to a signature is one thing, but with technology, platforms, and solutions providers changing so rapidly, it is highly likely that your contracts with data partners will be fulfilled in ways not originally contemplated in your agreements. Over the last decade, one great example of this has been the migration from file transfer "FTP" sites that transfer data files between parties to the use of application programming interfaces. Even as data transfer APIs sweep through the data world, there are issues with old contracts and agreements that were never updated to reflect the new realities of real-time data transfer.

Third, despite the greatest effort of security professionals to lock down their systems and data access, data leakage occurs through employees. Role-based access controls have offered one way to ensure that employees are only able to access the data or systems necessary to complete their job functions. Additionally, an internal data audit team can help you keep your own house in order, but the reality is that once your data is made available to a partner or reseller or customer, you have lost control of that same data. External hackers are a clear threat, but consider that in 2017, IBM found that more than two-thirds of all records compromised (and disclosed publicly) were due to "inadvertent insiders" — through mistakes made by employees.[32] So, with every data partnership, you must now be concerned with both your employees and the employees of your partner. Many of the insider incidents are not reported at all, as they tend to tarnish the reputation of the managers in charge of the insiders. Even the dreaded "cc: all," in which an employee accidentally sends courtesy copies to a huge list of customers, is a data leak by an insider. Under many of the new regulations, including the GDPR, you must report these situations.

For all of these reasons, your digital security approach requires the commitment of teams across your company. Your cybersecurity, internal access controls, and data audit teams need to be involved in your data partnership strategy to ensure that everyone is on the same page.

Data Partnership–Specific Approaches to Protecting Your Data

You should build specific elements related to data protection into your data partnership agreements. These explicit approaches help deter bad actors as well as keep even the most well-intentioned partners from straying later. Often, the people who create or negotiate a data partnership are not the individuals that will build the integration, oversee its deployment, or monitor the financial relationships it creates. And the longer a partnership is in place, the more likely it is that the people who set it up originally won't even work at those companies anymore. Because of this, you should use the tactics below to ensure the protection you intend for each partnership.

Contractual Agreement
It should go without saying, but too often, it doesn't: the contract you execute with your partners needs a thorough legal review, and depending

---

32   IBM Corporation, *IBM X-Force Threat Intelligence Index 2018*, March 2018, https://www-01.ibm.com/common/ssi/cgi-bin/ssialias?htmlfid=77014377USEN.

upon which data partnership structure you are entering into (mutually beneficial, innovator, or channel), your contract needs to preserve your ability to protect your data assets and your business reputation. Focus on the ways that data can and cannot be used rather than just the technical discussion surrounding the methods of delivery. Too many contracts in the data world spend inordinate amounts of verbiage on the data transfer method, because the IT department has hijacked the legal documentation. Remember, if it was FTP yesterday, and API integration now, in 10 years it could be — who knows? — a holographic handshake. The point is, your contract can state a mutually agreeable approach to data transfers, but it should focus far more on data usage, rights, and access.

In general, a data agreement should outline its specific purpose clearly. For example, you may be providing data for quality purposes, for matching purposes, or for the creation of a derivative dataset that combines your data with the partner's data. Each of these is an example of a specific use case that determines the partner's permissible use of the data. Be mindful, in particular, of derivative data rights, as covered chapter 8.

Next, focus upon the confidentiality of terms in the agreement, including pricing. The contract itself is confidential, but be sure the language specifically outlines how your relationship with each data partner is confidential.

With legislation like the GDPR, the California Consumer Privacy Act, and the wide array of regulatory requirements put in place each year, you must ensure that your data partners adhere to all applicable regulations as they handle your data, or you handle theirs. Going down with the ship is not a great strategy here, and we recommend that your DPO review your data partnership contracts as part of your company-wide dedication to compliance.

There are too many terms and potential caveats to name when discussing legal protections for your data partnership. That said, don't let your legal team or your partner's legal teams derail a great opportunity. The best attorneys we have worked with have been open and honest about their lack of topical knowledge when it comes to their clients' data, so they tend to accept their role as identifying the security and privacy issues and not necessarily the nitty-gritty detail of datasets or data security.

Contractual Reporting Rights

One of the best ways to ensure that a data partnership goes well is to incorporate mandatory reporting metrics into the contract. Specify the *minimum* number of fields; values or categories of data; and cadence needed to ensure that both parties are upholding the contract. Many data platforms, like app markets and reseller channels, have sophisticated reporting engines already built into their systems that allow for timely or even real-time reports on usage, access, and financial projections. Other partnerships include elements like data matching, appends, or crosswalked data connections that change as the two datasets you are aligning evolve. In those cases, you typically agree on an average number of records or a "high-water" mark for a given time period of usage, which would set out a usage maximum.

What do you need to confirm that the data partnership is working? You need agreed-upon parameters that outline success, including reporting on metrics like records viewed, fields downloaded, matches made, or customers signed. Your contracts should require a meeting between the two partners, at least quarterly and ideally face-to-face, to review the progress and reports from the partnership together. These meetings are well worth the effort and help to maintain a healthy relationship. Remember, there are no shortages of substitutes for datasets these days, so maintaining a transparent reporting regime with your partners through face-to-face meetings is imperative.

Jim Barksdale, CEO of the original browser company Netscape, said, "If we have data, let's look at data. If all we have are opinions, let's go with mine." We love this quote because it is so true. So many times, with new management or new relationships, opinions can crowd out the realities of a data partnership, so make sure that you build in contractual obligations to share all necessary reporting data.

Audit Rights

Companies dislike audits. Many a data partnership has died on this hill because one of the companies refused to give or get the right to audit their partners' use of their data. To be fair, a data audit is usually not nearly as difficult or intrusive as a financial or accounting audit, but many lawyers don't understand the difference. Depending upon the total value of the data partnership, audits may not be worth it. That said, the right to bring your data audit team to a partner to ask for simple access controls, use cases, and account verifications is reasonable, particularly in mutually beneficial data partnerships where the partners are of similar size and reputation.

Weigh the value of this right against the cost. You may find that a compromise is possible — not through a typical audit, but through the less disruptive right to scrape or crawl a partner's platform. Normally, the process of crawling and scraping, in which a partner uses a bot to read all the structured data on a page and stores it for their own use, is a touchy subject. In this case, you can get valuable insights from identifying the usage of your data within the partner's platform. We have seen this approach work to generate "audit-like" data on the usage of your data, so long as you agree not to retain other data gathered from the scrape.

Other Creative Protection Methods

Mystery shoppers and seed data are two methods that can help you protect your data assets. With mystery shopper rights, you are essentially asking for the right to pretend to be an interested prospect of your data partner's services. Although these rights don't have to be specifically outlined in a contract, we recommend that you add something to your agreement or at least let your partner know that you conduct these exercises. Companies are not fond of having their sales or service resources drained for someone who is only pretending to be interested. It's justifiable because the only real way to understand how a data partner is using your data or representing your data is by convincing their staff that they are pitching a real potential customer.

The second creative approach to data protection is the use of seed data. It should probably be called "weed" data because the whole point is to spread seeds in your data to see where those weeds pop up downstream. In this creative approach, you implant small amounts of fake data into your data files. This data is identifiably unique in its format; for example, a street address that doesn't exist, or a product description with your founder's name spelled backwards in it as an ingredient. The point of this fake data is that you can then search for these terms or unique data points in other databases and on other platforms, in much the same way that mapmakers used to insert false town names or geographic features into their maps to help identify if a competitor was selling a copy without a license. If you find your seed data in another database, then you can identify which partner you provided those particular seeds to, and work with that partner to find out how your seed data ended up on another platform without your consent.

You must build in contractual permission to include seed data; data partners do not take kindly to learning that you've been supplying them fake data. If you are delivering 1 million records and 24 of them are fake seed data, you should let your partners know you are doing that. Just don't tell them which records are fake.

Summarizing Data Protection

In the end, you will definitely be judged for how you protect your data. Your data, your customers' data, your partners' data: these will all haunt your dreams for years to come because nothing quite destroys shareholder value like a major data breach, leak, or inappropriate data sharing. The steps in the DataSmart Method are a great opportunity to prepare your company with the right approach and attitude toward data security and privacy. Many companies are using the new focus on data privacy laws, GDPR, and other DPA regulations as opportunities to overhaul their entire data strategy. As companies recognize that data privacy is not a fad and that data security breaches are inevitable, they also recognize the need to re-evaluate their commitment to data protection.

13

Summary and Conclusion

I N THIS CHAPTER, WE'LL provide an overall blueprint of the DataSmart Method for easy reference, along with some distilled analysis of how and why it is important. Use this section as a mini-index or a guide to help you when you're trying to recall a specific issue, scan for relevant topics, refresh your memory, or find a quick recap of a point you can relay to someone else. We'll also offer some forward-looking counsel about strategy, data protection, and thinking the right way about data. Our goal is to reaffirm some of the key points in the book, and also to give you actionable guidance about how to approach the data partnerships you have, or that you want to build.

Reviewing the DataSmart Method

Each of the four steps in the DataSmart Method represents an important component in any effort to build and sustain a business that effectively makes use of data. They also represent opportunities to think about the duality of your approach to data — that is, what *can* I do with this data and what *should* I do with this data. For instance, when you are valuing datasets, you have the chance also to consider whether the information you possess is worth the cost — financial, regulatory, figurative, and otherwise — of maintaining it, and maintaining it properly. And when deciding how best to protect your valuable data assets, you should conduct a meaningful analysis of whether you have the right personnel available to help you manage your data security and your data strategy.

The DataSmart Method, then, is both a practical approach to data strategy and a mindset. Here's a recap of the steps:

Identify
Identifying intrinsic and extrinsic data assets is crucial, because it is impossible to create partnerships that last without first understanding the data you have. In many ways, identification of data assets and datasets is the single most important aspect of building data partnerships, because an accurate understanding of the data at issue is a prerequisite for any other activity. This is why you must devote time and attention at the beginning to ensure that you capture all of the relevant information — intrinsic and extrinsic — that could be a part of your data strategy (see chapters 3 and 4). Approach the task with a healthy degree of skepticism about what you "know" your data assets to be. We can't count the number of times clients or customers have told us that they have only a few, limited datasets in their possession and then, after a few questions, the realization dawns that they have a massive amount of data they did not even consider. That realization is a large part of what the *Identify* step is about.

It is natural to want to move as quickly as possible from the identification of assets to their valuation and (potentially) sale, because the end goal of the entire process is to maximize value and grow. But as we've made clear, it is easy to overlook datasets that would augment, detract from, or complicate the usefulness of the partnerships you want to form. If your process isn't methodical, you can find yourself in a difficult position later, when assets you failed to identify are either claimed by your partner, excluded from a deal, or the subject of an unpleasant inquiry by a regulator.

That's why it is crucial to take the time necessary to completely identify your data assets. In chapter 3, we identified some mapping software and methods that are helpful in this process. Dedicated staff who are familiar with your datasets is also helpful, but there is no substitute for a thorough examination process. Meet with the most knowledgeable stakeholders to set parameters for data inflow mapping and potential data sources, and then follow up with subsequent meetings to update on progress and potential gaps in knowledge.

We also strongly recommend that you consult with your lawyer during this process, as identification is not only a component of your business plans but also a vital aspect of your data security and data compliance practice (see chapter 5). If your lawyer isn't data-oriented, then consider teaming your counsel with whomever you have designated as the company official in charge of privacy; either way, counsel needs to be involved in this process. Keeping your lawyer involved during the identification process provides a unique perspective on what sources of data to consider and how to classify them; for example, you may not have considered your offer letters to employees or their quarterly reviews to be a pertinent dataset, but your lawyer certainly might.

Finally, don't allow identification to become a one-time exercise. It's certainly true that the first time you conduct the exercise of identifying assets it will be a major undertaking, and will consume time and energy. But it need not be that complicated ever again, because, ideally, you will add to your inventory of data every time your company identifies a new dataset. Don't reinvent the wheel. Just add in new datasets as they arrive, and your company will be far more efficient in its data strategies and partnerships.

Value
Armed with your (regularly updated) inventory of datasets and sources, you will be well prepared to assign a value to data based on its present use or future potential use cases. Although it may seem counterintuitive, valuing datasets early in the process will serve you well. First, it ensures that you take a critical eye to any proposed use of your data, which will then guide your company to better understand how a partner might value it (see chapter 5). Next, you get the benefit of examining how your datasets interact with one another, and can take the opportunity to determine whether there is a more valuable use for data than how it is presently deployed. Finally, by estimating the value of the data, you can decide whether it is worth using or keeping at all, particularly given the emerging trend toward required data minimization.

Valuing assets early also ensures that you approach potential partners with a more realistic appraisal of your bargaining position and how to approach a negotiation. One notable benefit for negotiation is that you'll be armed with the right vocabulary. If you understand your exclusive rights to certain consumer data that's updated in real time and easily crosswalked across platforms, you're far more likely to make a compelling case for the value of that data than if you simply said, "We have data about what customers are buying."

In chapter 5, we explained how you can place virtually any dataset into one of four valuation buckets:

- $0 Bucket: Barter or Commoditized
- $10K Bucket: Valuable or Nascent
- $100K Bucket: Highly Valuable or Established
- $1M+ Bucket: Unique or Critical

These buckets are meant to quickly assign a value range, not an exact financial value, to your data assets. This is all about prioritizing the dataset against its peers and identifying where you should focus your partnership strategy. Additionally, the value range you ascribe to the data is a great way to identify assets that might require more protection or security. A highly valuable data asset may be worth encrypting, while a less valued dataset might be worth discarding systematically to align with data minimization standards. It all depends on how you calculate your risk-to-value ratio, a process with which your privacy professional and attorney can help.

Structure

Once you've completed the identification and valuation of your data assets, it's time to structure your partnership. This involves a substantial amount of legal work — everything from creating non-disclosure agreements to drafting contracts to forming business entities (see chapter 7). While your lawyer is a key player in all of this, typical legal copy-paste efforts won't work when it comes to data partnerships. Unless you ensure that your lawyer has a strong understanding both of your business model and your datasets, you may wind up with a business relationship that benefits your partner a lot more than it benefits you. Make sure that your lawyer understands the benefits of careful attention to the principles of the International Association of Privacy Professionals.

Assuming that you have good counsel, you will structure your relationship based on the best use case for your data and the smartest approach to maximize its value. These relationships take a variety of forms, of course, but they tend to fall into several primary categories (see chapter 8). These include the data quality partnership, the co-op, the innovator partnership, the reseller agreement, and the customer-driven reporting agreement. In chapter 8, we've summarized the primary forms of relationship for you and identified the challenges and problems that face each one.

Structure is important not only because it sets the rights and obligations of both sides, but also because how you enter into these relationships will determine how successful and profitable they will be for you. If you approach a relationship with a data partner without understanding that partner's likely goal, you're going to miss opportunities to maximize the value of the relationship.

Take the time to think through how much flexibility you will want during and especially at the end of the relationship (see chapter 9). You have to consider how you can exit the relationship, what data and rights you want to take with you, and how you intend to ensure that the valuable data assets you've brought to the arrangement don't wind up walking out the door with your partner. It may seem a little pessimistic to plan for the end of a relationship before it even begins, but it saves an enormous amount of stress later, and it gives your lawyer something to do.

Structuring data partnerships is about recognizing where your competencies lie and where you can tap into capabilities that your partners possess. If you consider every partnership as an opportunity to identify better use cases for data, better management platforms, or stronger oversight systems, you'll find that you derive more value from the relationship than appears on paper. Adaptation is critical for business success, and using these relationships for everything they're worth is essential to driving growth.

Protect
The last step of the DataSmart Method is also the longest-term effort: protecting data and protecting data subjects (see chapter 12). You need the right executives to protect your information. Data Protection Officers are a vital asset for companies that engage in widespread processing of

personal data, particularly those subject to the GDPR and similar regulatory frameworks. A team of professionals should support the DPO. They need the background and competency to conduct data audits, secure data, respond to regulators, manage data subject access requests, and handle the company's internal data practices.

Hiring a DPO is an optional measure for some companies, but determining who will be your primary point of contact and bear responsibility for data protection is not. All regulators, regardless of location, now expect that your company will dedicate resources to protect data, especially consumers' sensitive personal data. Failing to assign that responsibility to someone who understands it will simply compound the losses in the event of a data breach or data loss. In the inevitable investigations and lawsuits that follow, regulators and juries will surely pinpoint an ad hoc approach to data privacy as a critical flaw in the company's operations.

Data security is about much more than just passwords; it extends into a wide variety of activities designed to ensure the safety of information. In many ways, data security is a mindset that informs an operational approach. Of course, you should take the time to incorporate the best security measures you can and hire the best people to guide you, but at the same time, don't neglect the important work of rethinking how you bring in, analyze, process, store, and dispose of data. Those exercises are, ultimately, far more important, because they allow you to think creatively and critically about datasets in the same way that you did when you engaged in the *Identify* stage of this process.

Data security, like identification of datasets, is about an ongoing commitment to thinking about your data. Just as you need to take time to add new datasets to your inventory (and data brief) as they are created, you have to rethink your data security and data protection efforts every time you learn something new about your operations. Conduct social engineering tests to see if your employees understand how to spot a phishing scam. Consult with an expert to do a penetration test in which the consulting firm basically hacks your systems to identify weaknesses. With the help of your lawyer, conduct an internal, self-critical evaluation of your policies and procedures to understand your potential liabilities to data partners, customers, and regulators. In other words, dedicate the time and resources necessary to actually be smart when it comes to protecting your data.

Protect may be the last step of the DataSmart Method, but it is by no means the least. In many ways, it represents the most work over the longest period, because even after you've identified data, valued it, and structured its use in a partnership, you still need to protect the data and, importantly, the individuals who created it. It would be a mistake to forget that actual people underlie much of the data that businesses process, and actual people have enforceable rights to that data. Sometimes it is easier to think of data in the aggregate, disembodied from the people who entered it, or who it describes. But by remembering the actual individuals involved, you are less likely to engage in the kind of risky decision-making that leads to regulatory investigations or breaches. When you remember that data is about a person, you're less likely to do something like store personal health data and Social Security numbers in plain text on your computers at work.

We call our approach the DataSmart Method because we believe that when you *Identify*, *Value*, *Structure*, and *Protect* your data assets, you are following the best approach to managing data and forging ideal data partnerships. But we also call it a *method* because it's more about guidance than hard and fast rules. There will be times when you have to conduct a valuation before you've fully identified all data assets, or when expediency may force you to agree to a partnership structure that isn't ideal. Business is never clear-cut. Even so, you can always use this approach to establish the right process to leverage your data.

The Bigger Picture

Throughout this book, we've tried to give a broader perspective on why we advocate for a certain approach, or why we think our method makes sense. We outlined how important it is to approach partnerships with humility and leadership, and why forging the right relationships isn't just good practice but essential to functioning well in the data-driven market (see chapter 1). Data partnerships are becoming more challenging than traditional business arrangements because they necessarily involve third parties (either data subjects themselves or data aggregators). Your business must now deal with global data security regulations that are also evolving, bringing new obligations on users, creators, and processors of data.

Look beyond the straightforward questions of data processing and data ownership to think critically about the way data moves and affects business. You will sometimes still hear people talk about the "digital economy" or "data-based commerce," but we think those are anachronisms: it's all data now, and it's all digital now. Commerce is moving away from a simple producer-product-consumer framework to one where data drives production, data drives consumption, and data drives the analysis and sale of the data itself. If that sounds a little like an ouroboros (the snake swallowing itself), it should, because this process will not have a discernible start or end point. That's good; it means you can take advantage of data flows at any stage in the process, and learn to magnify your company's reach and appeal along with your value.

It also means that we need to be cautious. We need to harness the power of that data in a way that respects data subjects and recognizes how little we understand of the complicated processes used to analyze their data. The same data analysis that allows companies to provide us with more of what we want is also the data analysis that drives the content delivered to us. When Apple Music selects the "Music You'll Love" playlist this week, is it responding to your preferences or driving them? There's no satisfying answer to that question, but the mere fact of asking it is a central component of being mindful about data.[33]

In the same way, the complexity (and opacity) of machine learning and artificial intelligence mean that we will not be able to peer inside the box to understand how and why automated decisions are made. Arthur C. Clarke once wrote that any sufficiently advanced technology is indistinguishable from magic. If you've ever seen Google Assistant schedule a haircut appointment by saying "umm, sure" with a vaguely Valley accent,[34]

---

33   It also draws upon the ouroboros image again — algorithms have become so attuned to our desire for tailored goods that they are major contributors to the echo chamber effect in social media. This phenomenon, which was most widely commented upon during the 2016 US presidential election, has not abated (see "The Reason Your Feed Became an Echo Chamber, and What to Do about It," NPR, July 24, 2016, www.npr.org/sections/alltechconsidered/2016/07/24/486941582/the-reason-your-feed-became-an-echo-chamber-and-what-to-do-about-it).

34   Chris Welch, "Google Just Gave a Stunning Demo of Assistant Making an Actual Phone Call," The Verge, May 18, 2018, www.theverge.com/2018/5/8/17332070/google-assistant-makes-phone-call-demo-duplex-io-2018.

you'll understand what he meant. We have reached a point where the Turing test is becoming obsolete. APIs are connecting to one another on their own, and our ability to communicate with virtual assistants is moving from "What is the weather?" to "Overlay the weather for the next hour on our position, direction, velocity, and traffic, and tell us if we should stop for lunch now or later based upon available wait times at restaurants that are kid-friendly, highly rated, and have an allergy-friendly menu..."

This exciting future presents enormous opportunities to create value through data sharing partnerships. But we have to be thoughtful about how we create those partnerships, and recognize the need for controls that preserve our ability to interpose human checks on machine-based decision-making. That's why the GDPR includes a requirement that, before an automated decision is made, a human data subject has to consent, and has the right to inquire as to how the decision was reached. In the end, learning to be DataSmart is also about learning to be smart with someone else's data.

The DataSmart Method is a framework designed to prepare you to meet these future challenges and opportunities in data. By making sense of the data you have and how that data can be improved or of further value to others, you can unlock new growth opportunities and business models through data partnership.

Now, go leverage your data.

Index

About the Authors

CHRISTIAN J. WARD is currently the chief data officer of SourceMedia, in New York City, and an advisor to Ward PLLC on data strategy and partnerships.

With a background in creating and leading information and data companies, his focus is to help other businesses leverage their internal and external data as part of their overall business strategy by instituting the DataSmart Method. He has developed and executed hundreds of data partnerships around the world, from small entrepreneurial firms to the world's largest data companies.

Christian most recently was the executive vice president of data partnerships for Yext, the digital knowledge management platform based in New York. Before joining Yext, Christian was the chief data officer at Infogroup as well as the global head of content innovation at Thomson Reuters. He was managing director and director of research for Bank of New York (now BNY Mellon) and previously founded two different data companies, one in financial research and the other in media analytics. He has been quoted in the *Wall Street Journal*, *Forbes*, *Fortune*, *GeoMarketing*, *StreetFight*, and *Search Engine Journal*, and he speaks frequently on data strategy, partnerships, and the future influence of data.

Christian holds a BS in finance from the University of Florida.

JAMES J. WARD is the founder and managing partner of Ward PLLC, a law firm based in Miami.

Jay is an attorney and data security consultant. He provides his clients with counsel and advice on how to integrate intelligent, forward-looking policies and practices about data security into their daily operations — in other words, how to be data-smart. He also draws upon years of experience as a litigator in high-stakes disputes to provide insight into avoiding liability, and to zealously advocate for his clients when needed. He is the host of "DataSmart," a podcast on data security and strategy, and is frequently quoted in publications around the country, including the *Wall Street Journal*, *Forbes*, and the *International Business Times*.

Jay holds certifications in both European and United States data security and privacy law (CIPP/E and CIPP/US), as well as a certification in privacy program management (CIPM) from the International Association of Privacy Professionals, the only ISO/ANSI accredited body for data security and privacy.

His firm, Ward PLLC, provides clients with data security planning, GDPR compliance services, and legal counsel on data management and compliance issues, as well as handling litigation arising from or related to data breaches.

Before forming Ward PLLC, Jay was a litigator at elite international law firms in New York and Miami. He is a graduate of the University of Notre Dame Law School and Northwestern University.

Ward PLLC
Data Privacy Law | Data Strategy | DPO Services

1101 Brickell Avenue, 8th Floor
Miami, Florida 33131
www.wardpllc.com
email: info@wardpllc.com

50411781R00122

Made in the USA
Columbia, SC
06 February 2019